Better Homes and Gardens®
CALORIE COUNTER'S
COOK BOOK

© 1970 by Meredith Corporation, Des Moines, Iowa.
All Rights Reserved. Printed in the United States of America.
First Edition. Fifteenth Printing, 1980.
Library of Congress Catalog Card Number: 77-129266
ISBN: 0-696-00493-5

Contents

On the cover: Stuffed Cube Steak, Baked Stuffed Potato, lettuce salad, and Ambrosia comprise a slimming, yet satisfying menu. (See 1200 Calorie Menus, Day 1, page 68.)

At the left: Macaroni-Cheese Puff accompanied with Carrot-Orange Salad and fruit is an appealing menu that brightens any diet. (See 1500 Calorie Menus, Day 2, page 71.)

BETTER HOMES AND GARDENS® BOOKS

Editorial Director: Don Dooley
Managing Editor: Malcolm E. Robinson Art Director: John Berg
Asst. Managing Editor: Lawrence D. Clayton
Asst. Art Director: Randall Yontz
Food Editor: Nancy Morton
Senior Food Editor: Joyce Trollope
Associate Editors: Lorene Mundhenke, Sharyl Heiken,
Rosemary Corsiglia
Assistant Editors: Pat Olson, Sandra Mapes,
Elizabeth Strait, Catherine Penney, Elizabeth Walter
Designers: George Meininger, Harijs Priekulis, Faith Berven

FOREWORD

"I gotta go on a diet" is usually punctuated with a groan or a long exclamation mark twisted into the word "ugh." This should not be the case and certainly won't be if the approach chosen is the one outlined in this book. Dieting, you see, is really a way of life. Some folks can eat like the proverbial horse and look as though they regularly dined on sautéed butterfly antennae. Unfortunately, controlling weight isn't like that for most of us. We are counting the illusive calorie either to stay slim or to lose weight. Generally, we wish the calorie were more elusive.

There are many psychological approaches to weight control, ranging from "By gum, I'm gonna do it this time," to "If I understood why I gained weight and maintained it, I would be better equipped to lose it." No weight loss program will be successful unless the dieter is positively motivated. Motivation can come in a number of ways, but none is stronger than that which originates within the individual—the individual who takes pride in how he looks and feels—unless, that is, he has had the living daylights scared out of him by his physician. Now *that* can induce motivation.

The physician is concerned about overweight because of the generally poor health records of overweight people. People who are grossly overweight belong to a statistical fraction of the population which suffers more often from diabetes and heart and kidney disease, for example, than does the lean statistical fraction. What's more, the overweight segment usually presents a greater risk in the event of surgery; furthermore, they don't live as long either. So you see, there are health reasons as well as personal reasons for slimming down.

The physician is also concerned about his patients' cholesterol levels, particularly if a patient shows a tendency to accumulate fats in the blood (hyperlipidemia). These people are usually advised to avoid dietary sources of cholesterol and to keep the total intake of fat to a minimum. This task is accomplished easily whether you are on a diet or not, and this book's chart will help those on a low-cholesterol diet.

Most physicians become alarmed when their patients try out crash diets because such regimens can tax the body when dealing with the metabolic idiosyncrasies generated by these nonsensical approaches. It is always desirable to have regular physical examinations, especially if one is overweight or has been unfortunate in his choice of grand-parents. Before initiating a major job of overhauling one's body contours, it would be well to start off with an examination.

Calories, calories. The word is used endlessly until it seems that food is nothing but a writhing mass of calories. The great number of calorie tables attests to this. Foods should be selected on the basis of nutrient content and personal preference, not solely on their caloric contribution. Unless one has expert help, it is easy to make nutritional "boo-boos" if the calorie content of food is the main criterion for selection. That is where *The Calorie Counter's Cook Book* enters the picture. Much of the nutritional planning has been done for you.

This book contains many splendid examples of tasty and attractive dishes with lots of recipes and menu ideas. It truly represents a calorie counter's guidebook to paradise. Good food, attractively presented, is a boon to the calorie-conscious dieter interested in making a long-range change in food patterns. And that's what dieting is all about. Learning while losing. Learning a new way of life that will assure continuation of the hard-earned, svelte new figure.

Philip L. White, Sc. D.
Secretary
Council of Foods and Nutrition
American Medical Association

This seal is your warranty that every recipe in this book has been tested for family appeal, practicality, and deliciousness, and is endorsed by the Better Homes and Gardens Test Kitchen.

Acknowledgement: Many of the calorie counts throughout this book are based upon information obtained from *Composition of Foods*, by Bernice K. Watt and Annabel L. Merrill (Washington, D.C., Agriculture Handbook Number 8, United States Department of Agriculture, 1963); and from *Food Values of Portions Commonly Used*, by Anna dePlanter Bowes and Charles F. Church (Tenth Edition, Philadelphia, J. P. Lippincott Co., 1966).

Calorie-Trimmed Recipes

Do you lose interest faster
than weight when you diet? If so,
you'll be pleased with this tempting
assortment of mouth-watering,
calorie-counted recipes
that will keep your interest high
while you shed those extra
pounds. Within this section you'll
find an appealing array
of appetizers, main dishes,
vegetables, salads, sandwiches,
desserts, and beverages
geared to the dieter
who enjoys food at its best.

**Alternate layers of fresh
fruit with a banana-yogurt mixture
for cool and inviting
Honeydew - Berry Parfaits.**

LOW-CALORIE APPETIZERS AND SNACKS

MUSHROOM COCKTAIL

38 calories/serving

Bright and zesty cocktail sauce is a natural for other appetizers and seafood courses—

- ⅓ cup catsup
- 1 tablespoon vinegar
- ¼ teaspoon prepared horseradish
  Lettuce leaves
- 1½ cups lettuce, shredded
- 12 fresh medium mushrooms, sliced

In small bowl blend catsup, vinegar, and horseradish. Chill. Line 6 sherbets with lettuce leaves; layer with shredded lettuce. Arrange about ¼ cup sliced mushrooms atop each. Chill. Just before serving, drizzle with 1 tablespoon catsup mixture. Makes 6 servings.

SPICED CITRUS APPETIZER CUP

52 calories/serving

Whet appetites with this tasty orange-grapefruit appetizer cup. Make it ahead, serve chilled, and watch your guests enjoy it—

- 1 16-ounce can mixed grapefruit and orange sections, undrained (2 cups)
- 3 inches stick cinnamon
  Dash ground cloves
  Dash ground ginger

In saucepan combine grapefruit and orange sections, cinnamon stick, cloves, and ginger; simmer for 10 minutes. Remove cinnamon stick. Chill. Serve in sherbets. Garnish with mint sprig, if desired. Makes 5 servings.

An elegant beginning

←Set a trend by serving a delicious and unusual first course appetizer in your prettiest stemware. Make it a Mushroom Cocktail.

GRAPEFRUIT-CRAB COCKTAIL

57 calories/serving

Another time substitute lobster for crab—

- 1 7½-ounce can crab meat, chilled, drained, flaked, and cartilage removed
- 1 tablespoon lemon juice
- 1 16-ounce can unsweetened grapefruit segments, chilled
- ⅓ cup catsup
- ¼ teaspoon dry mustard
- ¼ teaspoon prepared horseradish
  Dash bottled hot pepper sauce
  Lettuce

Sprinkle crab with lemon juice. Drain grapefruit, reserving ¼ cup juice. Combine catsup, ¼ cup reserved grapefruit juice, dry mustard, horseradish, and hot pepper sauce; chill. Arrange grapefruit and crab in lettuce-lined sherbets. Drizzle with sauce. Makes 8 servings.

FROSTY FRUIT CUP

66 calories/serving

The surprise is the tasty lemon-lime slush—

- 1 15-ounce can pineapple chunks (juice pack)
- 1 16-ounce bottle low-calorie lemon-lime carbonated beverage
- 2 tablespoons lime juice
  Few drops green food coloring
- 1 cup seedless green grapes
- 2 cups cantaloupe balls

Drain pineapple, reserving juice. Combine reserved juice, carbonated beverage, lime juice, and food coloring; stir. Pour into 3-cup refrigerator tray; freeze just to a mush, about 2 to 2½ hours. Combine fruits. Break frozen mixture apart with fork, if necessary. Spoon into 8 sherbet glasses; top with fruits. Trim with mint sprigs, if desired. Makes 8 servings.

CURRIED CHICKEN SOUP

61 calories / serving

Delicious served either hot or cold—

    1 10½-ounce can condensed cream of
         chicken soup
    1¼ cups skim milk
    ½ cup water
    ½ teaspoon curry powder
    1 tablespoon snipped parsley

In small saucepan gradually stir milk into soup. Add remaining ingredients. Heat till simmering, stirring occasionally. Garnish with additional snipped parsley, if desired. Serves 6.

FRENCH ONION SOUP

42 calories / serving

A low-calorie version of a favorite soup—

    1 large onion, thinly sliced (1 cup)
    1 tablespoon butter or margarine
    2 10½-ounce cans condensed beef broth
    ¾ cup water
    ½ teaspoon Worcestershire sauce
       Dash pepper
    1 tablespoon grated Parmesan cheese

Cook onion in butter over medium-low heat till lightly browned, about 20 minutes. Add beef broth, water, and Worcestershire. Bring to boiling; season with pepper. Pour into bowls; sprinkle with cheese. Makes 7 servings.

HERBED TOMATO BROTH

22 calories / serving

Hot tomato starter with marjoram and thyme—

    1 10½-ounce can condensed beef broth
    1 cup tomato juice
    ¼ teaspoon dried marjoram leaves,
         crushed
    ¼ teaspoon dried thyme leaves, crushed
    1 tablespoon snipped parsley

Combine beef broth, tomato juice, ¾ cup water, marjoram, and thyme. Heat to boiling. Reduce heat and simmer 2 minutes. Ladle into bowls. Garnish with parsley. Makes 6 servings.

Enjoy Marinated Sprouts as a between-meal nibble, or serve to guests as an hors d'oeuvre for enjoyable low-calorie snacking.

MARINATED SPROUTS

13 calories / appetizer

Sprouts take on a delightful dill flavor—

Cook one 10-ounce package frozen Brussels sprouts according to package directions; drain. Cut large pieces in half. Combine ½ cup low-calorie Italian salad dressing; 1 small clove garlic, minced; 2 tablespoons finely chopped onion; 1 teaspoon dried parsley flakes; and ½ teaspoon dried dillweed. Pour over warm Brussels sprouts. Cover; marinate in refrigerator for several hours or overnight. Drain; serve with cocktail picks. Makes 2 cups.

TOMATO-CRAB BITES

16 calories / appetizer

Use a bed of chipped ice to hold tiny tomato appetizers upright for easy serving—

Blend ¼ cup low-calorie mayonnaise-type dressing, 1 teaspoon lemon juice, ¼ teaspoon salt, and few drops bottled hot pepper sauce. Stir in 2 tablespoons chopped green onion and one 7½-ounce can crab meat, drained, cartilage removed, and chopped. Hollow out 1 pint (25 to 30) cherry tomatoes. Stuff tomatoes with crab mixture. Makes about 30 appetizers.

PICKLED SHRIMP
27 calories / appetizer

Make these peppy appetizers in advance and save time for party fun—

    1 pound fresh or frozen shrimp
        in shells
 ¼ cup celery leaves
    2 tablespoons mixed pickling spices
 1½ teaspoons salt
 ½ cup sliced onion
    4 bay leaves
 ¾ cup low-calorie Italian salad
        dressing
 ⅛ cup white vinegar
    1 tablespoon capers with liquid
    1 teaspoon celery seed
 ½ teaspoon salt
      Few drops bottled hot pepper sauce

Cover shrimp with boiling water; add celery leaves, pickling spices, and 1½ teaspoons salt. Cover and simmer for 5 minutes. Drain; peel and devein shrimp under cold water. Mix shrimp, onion, and bay leaves; arrange in shallow dish. Combine remaining ingredients; mix well. Pour over shrimp mixture. Cover; marinate in refrigerator at least 24 hours, spooning marinade over shrimp occasionally. Makes about 2½ cups pickled shrimp and onions.

Pop Artichoke-Ham Bites into the oven as the party begins and wait for the enticing aroma to attract guests to the snack tray.

LOW-CALORIE

COOKING TIP

No need to serve high-calorie dips when appetizers, such as shrimp, are marinated in low-calorie dressings. Spoon marinade over individual appetizers to develop full flavor.

DILLED VEGETABLE STICKS
89 calories / cup

Enjoy crisp, dill-flavored vegetable sticks for evening snacking—

Snip ends from 1 pound fresh green beans and wash thoroughly; leave whole. Cook in boiling, salted water till crisp-tender, about 5 minutes. Drain. Peel 1 pound carrots and cut into thin sticks. Cook in boiling, salted water till crisp-tender, about 3 minutes. Drain. Combine vegetables. Add 2 teaspoons dried dillweed, 2 teaspoons mustard seed, and 4 cloves garlic, halved. In saucepan combine 2½ cups water, 1 cup vinegar, and ½ cup sugar; bring to boiling. Pour over vegetables. Cool; cover and chill overnight. Vegetables may be stored for 2 weeks in refrigerator. Makes 8 cups.

ARTICHOKE-HAM BITES
20 calories / appetizer

An elegant, sizzling snack idea—

    1 14-ounce can artichoke hearts
 ½ cup low-calorie Italian salad
        dressing
 ⅛ teaspoon garlic powder
    6 slices boiled ham

Drain artichoke hearts; cut in half. Combine dressing and garlic powder; add artichokes. Marinate several hours; drain. Cut ham into 1x4-inch strips. Wrap one strip around each artichoke half. Secure with wooden pick. Bake at 300° about 10 minutes. Makes 24.

Surround flavorful Cheesy-Herb Dip with a vegetable medley of sliced cauliflowerets, carrot skewers, and thin celery sticks.

TUNA BALLS
16 calories / appetizer

Tangy nuggets of tuna and cheese rolled in snipped parsley are fun to eat with a fancy cocktail pick—

- 1 7-ounce can water-pack tuna, drained and flaked
- 1 3-ounce package Neufchatel cheese
- 2 tablespoons finely chopped celery
- 2 teaspoons lemon juice
- ½ teaspoon Worcestershire sauce
- ¼ teaspoon salt
- ⅛ cup finely snipped parsley

Blend tuna and cheese. Add celery, lemon juice, Worcestershire, and salt; mix well. Allowing 2 teaspoons for each, form mixture into small balls. Roll in parsley. Chill well. Serve with cocktail picks. Makes about 30.

DEVILED EGGS
47 calories / appetizer

Cottage cheese cuts calories in the filling—

Halve 6 hard-cooked eggs lengthwise; remove yolks. In blender container combine yolks with ¼ cup cream-style cottage cheese, 2 tablespoons skim milk, 1 tablespoon snipped parsley, 1 teaspoon vinegar, 1 teaspoon prepared mustard, ¼ teaspoon salt, ¼ teaspoon prepared horseradish, and dash pepper. Blend at medium speed till mixture is smooth. Stop blender and scrape sides occasionally. Spoon yolk mixture into egg whites; garnish with additional snipped parsley, if desired. Makes 12.

CHEESY-HERB DIP
22 calories / tablespoon

Flavored just right with herbs and seasonings—

- 1 cup low-calorie mayonnaise-type dressing
- 1 3-ounce package Neufchatel cheese, softened
- 1 teaspoon mixed salad herbs, crushed
- ¼ teaspoon salt
- 1 tablespoon snipped parsley
- 1 tablespoon grated onion
- ½ teaspoon Worcestershire sauce
- 2 teaspoons capers, drained

Blend all ingredients and chill well. Serve as a dip for carrot sticks, celery sticks, and sliced cauliflowerets. Makes 1½ cups.

ZESTY ZUCCHINI DIP
25 calories / tablespoon

Serve with melba toast or vegetable dippers—

In a saucepan combine 2 cups diced zucchini (2 medium); 1 tablespoon chopped onion; ½ cup tomato juice; ½ teaspoon salt; and ⅛ teaspoon dried basil leaves, crushed. Simmer, covered, 20 minutes. Put in blender container; add one 8-ounce package Neufchatel cheese, cubed. Cover; blend on high speed till mixture is smooth. Remove from blender; chill. Just before serving, stir 1 tablespoon bacon-flavored bits into chilled mixture. Makes about 1⅔ cups.

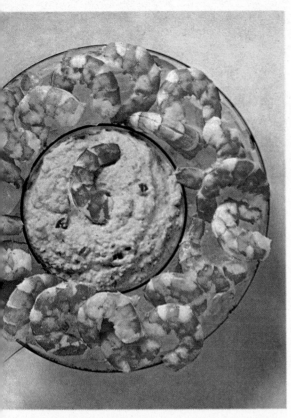

Even non-dieters will enjoy tempting Dieter's Dip served with chilled cooked shrimp arranged on a bed of chipped ice.

SCALLOPS WITH DIP
20 calories / tablespoon

Chilled shrimp make excellent dippers also—

> 1 12-ounce package frozen scallops (not breaded), thawed
> 1 8-ounce carton yogurt
> ¼ cup catsup
> 1 small sweet pickle, finely chopped
> ½ teaspoon prepared mustard

Place scallops and 1 tablespoon salt in 2 cups boiling water. Cover; return to boiling. Reduce heat; simmer 3 to 4 minutes. Drain. Cut large scallops in half; chill thoroughly.

To prepare dip, combine yogurt with catsup, pickle, mustard, and ½ teaspoon salt in small bowl; mix well. Chill. Serve with chilled scallops. Makes about 1¼ cups.

Low-calorie dippers include vegetables, fruits, and seafood

Use low-calorie mayonnaise-type dressing, yogurt, cottage cheese, or Neufchatel cheese to save calories when making party dips.

DIETER'S DIP
15 calories / tablespoon

A good companion with seafood appetizers—

Beat together with electric mixer one 12-ounce carton cream-style cottage cheese (1½ cups) and ½ envelope dill dip mix (about 1 teaspoon). Stir in 1 tablespoon finely diced pimiento and 1 tablespoon snipped parsley. Serve with chilled, cooked shrimp. Makes about 1½ cups.

PARTY CHEESE DIP
29 calories / tablespoon

Also delicious served as a salad dressing—

> 1 5-ounce jar Neufchatel cheese spread with pimiento
> 1 cup dry cottage cheese
> 3 tablespoons skim milk
> 1 teaspoon prepared horseradish
> Several drops bottled hot pepper sauce

Combine all ingredients; beat till thoroughly blended and fluffy. Chill. Serve with raw vegetables or cooked shrimp. Makes 1¼ cups.

QUICK FRUIT DIP
9 calories / tablespoon

Vary low-calorie jam for different flavor—

Combine one 8-ounce carton yogurt, 3 tablespoons low-calorie strawberry jam, and ¼ teaspoon ground cinnamon; chill. Serve with chilled fruit dippers: seedless green grapes, apple wedges, cantaloupe or honeydew balls, or pineapple chunks. Makes about 1¼ cups.

SLIMMING MAIN DISHES

STUFFED CUBE STEAKS

252 calories / serving

As pictured on front cover—

    6 beef cube steaks (1¾ pounds)
      Salt
      Pepper
    ½ cup low-calorie French-style
        salad dressing
    1 cup shredded carrot
    ¾ cup finely chopped onion
    ¾ cup finely chopped green pepper
    ¾ cup finely chopped celery
    ½ cup canned beef broth
    4 teaspoons cornstarch
    ¼ teaspoon kitchen bouquet

Pound steaks to ¼-inch thickness. Sprinkle generously with salt and pepper; brush with salad dressing. Place in shallow dish; marinate for 30 to 60 minutes at room temperature.

In saucepan combine carrot, onion, green pepper, celery, ¼ cup water, and ¼ teaspoon salt. Simmer, covered, till vegetables are crisp-tender, about 7 to 8 minutes. Drain.

Place about ⅓ cup vegetable mixture on each steak. Roll up jelly-roll fashion; secure with wooden picks. Place meat rolls in 10-inch skillet; pour beef broth over. Simmer, covered, till tender, about 35 to 40 minutes.

Transfer meat to serving platter; remove picks. Skim fat from broth; reserve ¾ cup broth. Blend cornstarch with 2 tablespoons cold water; stir into reserved broth. Cook and stir till thick and bubbly; stir in kitchen bouquet. Pour over steak rolls. Makes 6 servings.

LOW-CALORIE

Broil or roast meat to reduce main dish calories

COOKING TIP

Use a metal rack when broiling or roasting to allow fat to escape. As the meat cooks, the fat slowly bastes and seasons the meat.

DEVILED STEAK

215 calories / serving

Flame steak in chafing dish at the table—

    1½ pounds beef sirloin steak,
        1 inch thick
    2 tablespoons butter or margarine
    1 tablespoon snipped parsley
    1 tablespoon dry sherry
    1 teaspoon dry mustard
    1 teaspoon Worcestershire sauce
    2 tablespoons warm brandy
    ¼ cup catsup
    1 4-ounce can sliced mushrooms,
        drained

Trim excess fat from meat. Broil 3 inches from heat for 5 to 6 minutes on each side; steak will be rare. In large skillet combine butter, next 4 ingredients, ¼ teaspoon salt, and dash pepper; heat till bubbly. Add steak; pour brandy over. Flame. When brandy has burned down, remove steak. Add catsup and mushrooms to skillet; mix well. Serve over steak. Serves 6.

ONION-SMOTHERED STEAK

231 calories / serving

A new version of a popular steak—

    1½ pounds beef round steak,
        ¾ inch thick
    ¼ cup all-purpose flour
    2 tablespoons shortening
    3 medium onions, sliced
    1 tablespoon vinegar
    1 clove garlic, minced
    1 bay leaf
    ¼ teaspoon dried thyme leaves, crushed

Trim excess fat from meat. Combine flour, 1 teaspoon salt, and ⅛ teaspoon pepper; pound into meat. Cut in serving-size pieces. Brown in hot shortening; drain off fat. Top with onion; stir in 1 cup water and remaining ingredients. Bring to boiling; reduce heat. Simmer, covered, 1 hour. Remove bay leaf. Makes 6 servings.

PEPPER STEAK

202 calories / serving

Another time serve this peppy entrée over rice—

1½ pounds beef round steak,
    ½ inch thick
1 tablespoon shortening
1 16-ounce can tomato wedges
½ medium onion, thinly sliced
1 small clove garlic, minced
2 teaspoons beef-flavored gravy base
1 teaspoon Worcestershire sauce
¼ teaspoon salt
2 medium green peppers, cut in
    ½-inch strips

Trim excess fat from steak; cut meat into 2x¼-inch strips. In medium skillet brown meat strips in hot shortening; drain off excess fat. Drain tomatoes, reserving liquid.

Add reserved tomato liquid, onion slices, garlic clove, beef-flavored gravy base, Worcestershire sauce, salt, and dash pepper to browned meat strips. Cover tightly and simmer mixture over low heat for 50 minutes.

Stir in green pepper strips and tomato wedges. Cook meat mixture, covered, till green pepper is tender, about 6 to 8 minutes.

Remove meat and vegetables to serving bowl with slotted spoon. Reserve cooking liquid to pass, adding additional hot water to make ½ cup, if necessary. Makes 6 servings.

Meat entrées such as Deviled Steak and Onion-Smothered Steak make calorie counting a pleasure. Complete the menu with a vegetable, a crisp-green salad, dessert, and beverage.

ITALIAN VEAL CUTLETS

250 calories / serving

Cutlets simmer in a peppy, tomato-caper sauce—

- 4 boneless veal cutlets (1 pound)
- 2 teaspoons shortening
- 1 8-ounce can tomatoes, cut up
- 1 teaspoon Worcestershire sauce
- 1 tablespoon snipped parsley
- 2 teaspoons capers, drained
- ¼ teaspoon garlic salt
- ¼ teaspoon dried oregano leaves, crushed

Pound veal to ¼- to ⅛-inch thickness or have meatman tenderize cutlets. Brown quickly in hot shortening. Blend remaining ingredients; add to meat. Cover; simmer 35 to 40 minutes. Uncover; simmer till tender, about 10 minutes. To serve, spoon sauce over meat. Serves 4.

OVEN-STYLE SWISS STEAK

171 calories / serving

Perfect main dish for a busy day at home—

- 2 pounds beef round steak, 1 inch thick
- 1 teaspoon salt
- ¼ teaspoon pepper
- 1 medium onion, sliced (½ cup)
- 1 4-ounce can sliced mushrooms, drained
- 1 8-ounce can tomato sauce

Trim fat from meat. Pound meat with meat mallet; sprinkle with salt and pepper. Place meat in 11¾x7½x1¾-inch baking dish. Top with onion and mushrooms; pour sauce over all. Cook, covered, at 350° for 1½ hours. Uncover; cook 15 minutes longer. Baste occasionally. To serve, spoon sauce over meat. Serves 8.

SEASONING GUIDE FOR MEATS

Spices and herbs add flavor to meat, fish, and poultry without adding calories. Experiment with different seasonings by adding ¼ teaspoon dried herb for each 4 servings. Increase the amount of herb or spice if more seasoning is desired. To use dried herbs in leaf form, measure and then crush before adding to meat. To use fresh herbs, use 3 times more of the seasoning and snip, rather than crush. Use fresh herbs when available.

Beef	allspice, basil, bay leaf, caraway seed, celery seed, chili powder, cumin, curry powder, dill, garlic, ginger, mace, marjoram, mustard, oregano, rosemary, savory, tarragon, thyme
Fish and Shellfish	basil, bay leaf, cardamom, celery seed, chili powder, cumin, curry powder, dill, fennel, garlic, marjoram, mustard, oregano, paprika, rosemary, saffron, sage, savory, tarragon, thyme
Ham	allspice, cloves, cinnamon, coriander, curry powder, ginger, mustard
Lamb	allspice, basil, bay leaf, caraway seed, curry powder, dill, garlic, ginger, marjoram, mint, oregano, rosemary, sage, savory, thyme
Pork	basil, caraway seed, cloves, garlic, ginger, marjoram, mustard, nutmeg, oregano, paprika, rosemary, sage, savory, thyme
Poultry	basil, bay leaf, celery seed, chili powder, cumin, curry powder, dill, garlic, ginger, marjoram, mustard, oregano, paprika, rosemary, saffron, sage, savory, tarragon, thyme
Veal	anise, basil, bay leaf, curry powder, ginger, mace, marjoram, mint, mustard, oregano, rosemary, sage, savory, thyme

Calorie-low marinades add flavor to meat. Pour marinade over meat in plastic bag and close. Press bag to distribute marinade.

BARBECUED CHUCK ROAST

291 calories / serving

Next time grill outdoors over glowing charcoal—

Trim fat from one 3-pound chuck roast, 1½ to 2 inches thick. Place meat in clear plastic bag; set in deep bowl. Mix ⅓ cup wine vinegar, ¼ cup catsup, 2 tablespoons soy sauce, 1 teaspoon salt, 2 teaspoons Worcestershire sauce, 1 teaspoon prepared mustard, ¼ teaspoon garlic powder, and ¼ teaspoon pepper.

Pour over meat; close bag. Marinate 2 to 3 hours at room temperature or overnight in refrigerator. Turn bag occasionally to distribute marinade. Remove meat from bag; reserve marinade. Place meat on rack of broiler pan. Broil 6 to 8 inches from heat till medium rare, about 50 to 60 minutes; turn meat every 10 minutes. Baste with reserved marinade the last 15 to 20 minutes. Makes 8 servings.

LIVER WITH MUSHROOMS

181 calories / serving

Simple marinade is a low-calorie salad dressing—

Marinate one 4-ounce can sliced mushrooms, drained, in ⅓ cup low-calorie French-style salad dressing for 30 minutes. Meanwhile, remove membrane from 1 pound calves liver, ½ inch thick; cut in serving-size pieces.

Drain mushrooms, reserving marinade. Brush both sides of liver with reserved marinade. Broil 3 inches from heat for 4 minutes. Turn; top with mushrooms. Broil till liver is tender, about 4 minutes longer. Makes 4 servings.

MARINATED POT ROAST

260 calories / serving

Flavor is reminiscent of sauerbraten—

    1 3-pound heel of round beef roast
    1 cup pineapple juice
    ½ cup red wine vinegar
    1 medium onion, sliced
    1 clove garlic, minced
    2 bay leaves
    2 teaspoons Worcestershire sauce
    2 tablespoons all-purpose flour

Trim excess fat from roast. Place meat in clear plastic bag; set in deep bowl. Mix juice, next 5 ingredients, ½ cup water, 2 teaspoons salt, and ¼ teaspoon pepper. Pour over meat; close bag. Marinate overnight in refrigerator. Occasionally turn bag to distribute marinade.

Transfer roast from bag to Dutch oven. Strain marinade; reserve 1 cup liquid. Add strained onion, bay leaves, and reserved liquid to meat. Cover tightly; simmer for 2¼ to 2½ hours. Remove meat. Skim fat from pan juices; reserve 1 cup juices. Remove bay leaves. Mix flour with ¼ cup cold water; add to reserved juices. Cook and stir till bubbly; cook and stir 2 to 3 minutes more. Spoon over meat. Serves 8.

Vary the pot roast routine with Barbecued Chuck Roast. Marinate roast in tangy tomato sauce to tenderize meat before broiling.

BROILED BEEF FILLETS

184 calories / serving

Wine marinade makes these steaks exceptional—

- ½ cup claret
- 2 tablespoons soy sauce
- ½ cup finely chopped onion
- 2 tablespoons finely snipped parsley
- 1 clove garlic, minced
  Dash pepper
- 4 4-ounce beef tenderloin fillets,
    1 inch thick

Combine first 6 ingredients. Place fillets in plastic bag; pour wine marinade over fillets. Close bag. Marinate 2 hours in refrigerator; press bag occasionally to distribute marinade. Remove fillets from bag; reserve marinade. Broil steaks 3 inches from heat for 7 minutes. Turn; broil 6 minutes longer or to desired degree of doneness. Remove to warm serving platter.

Heat reserved marinade to boiling; spoon over broiled fillets. Makes 4 servings.

MARINATED BEEF KABOBS

219 calories / serving

Skewered vegetables and meat cook quickly—

- ½ envelope dry onion soup mix (¼ cup)
- 1 beef bouillon cube
- 1 teaspoon prepared horseradish
- ¼ teaspoon paprika
- 1 pound beef sirloin
- 12 fresh large mushrooms
- 2 medium tomatoes, cut in sixths

Combine first 4 ingredients and ¾ cup water; bring to boiling. Reduce heat; simmer 5 minutes. Cool. Trim fat from meat; cut in 1-inch cubes. Add meat and mushrooms to marinade; toss to coat. Cover; marinate in refrigerator several hours or overnight. Drain; reserve marinade. Thread skewers alternately with meat, mushrooms, and tomatoes. Broil 3 inches from heat, 5 to 6 minutes; brush with reserved marinade. Turn; broil 4 to 5 minutes longer. Brush with marinade. Makes 4 servings.

Highlight summertime picnics with Hawaiian Ham Slices. Before leaving home, marinate ham in ginger-soy marinade. When mealtime arrives, grill ham and pineapple over portable grill.

LOW-CALORIE COOKING TIP

Trim excess fat from meat before cooking to reduce calories. Use a sharp knife to remove fat from steaks, chops, and roasts.

HAWAIIAN HAM SLICES

238 calories / serving

Use juice from canned pineapple in marinade—

Trim excess fat from 1 pound fully cooked boneless ham; slice into 4 portions. Blend ⅓ cup pineapple juice; 2 tablespoons soy sauce; ¾ teaspoon ground ginger; and ½ clove garlic, minced. Pour over ham in shallow container. Marinate 30 minutes, turning once.

Remove ham from marinade; reserve marinade. Grill over *hot* coals till heated through, about 2 minutes on each side. Brush often with reserved marinade. Heat 4 canned pineapple slices (juice pack) on grill during last 2 minutes. Serve pineapple atop ham. Serves 4.

PEACH-SAUCED HAM

217 calories / serving

Orange juice and cloves accent peach sauce—

Trim excess fat from 1 fully cooked ham slice, 1 inch thick (about 2 pounds); slash ham edges at 1-inch intervals. Place on broiler pan. Broil 3 inches from heat for 7 to 8 minutes; turn. Broil 5 to 6 minutes longer.

Meanwhile, drain one 16-ounce can dietetic pack peach slices, reserving ½ cup liquid. In saucepan blend reserved peach liquid with 1 tablespoon cornstarch and ¼ teaspoon ground cloves. Stir in 1 teaspoon shredded orange peel and ½ cup orange juice. Cook, stirring constantly, till mixture thickens and bubbles; add peach slices. Heat through. Serve peach sauce atop ham. Makes 8 servings.

LONDON BROIL

188 calories / serving

Lemon pepper adds a subtle flavor—

Score 1½ pounds top-quality beef flank steak on both sides. Place in shallow pan. Blend ¾ cup low-calorie Italian salad dressing, 2 tablespoons soy sauce, ⅛ teaspoon onion juice, and ⅛ teaspoon lemon pepper; pour over steak. Cover. Let stand at room temperature for 2 to 3 hours; turn several times. Place steak on rack of broiler pan. Broil 3 inches from heat for 5 minutes; season with salt. Turn; broil 5 minutes more for medium rare. Season with salt. Carve broiled steak in *very thin* slices diagonally across grain. Makes 6 servings.

PINEAPPLE-PORK CHOPS

240 calories / serving

Golden pineapple sauce accents the pork—

Trim fat from 6 loin pork chops (2 pounds); reserve trimmings. In skillet heat trimmings till 1 tablespoon fat accumulates; discard trimmings. Brown chops on both sides in hot fat; drain. Season with salt and pepper.

Drain one 20-ounce can pineapple chunks (juice pack), reserving ½ cup juice. Mix reserved juice, 1 tablespoon brown sugar, and pineapple chunks. Arrange ½ medium onion, thinly sliced, over chops; top with pineapple. Cover; simmer for 50 to 60 minutes. Remove chops; skim fat from skillet. Blend 2 teaspoons cornstarch with 1 tablespoon cold water; stir into skillet. Cook and stir till thick and bubbly. Serve pineapple sauce over chops. Serves 6.

ORANGE-GLAZED LAMB

350 calories / serving

Orange marmalade provides a jiffy glaze—

Trim excess fat from 8 loin chops, cut ¾ inch thick (about 2 pounds). Season chops with salt. Broil 3 to 4 inches from heat, 6 to 8 minutes. Turn; broil 4 minutes more. Combine ¼ cup low-calorie orange marmalade and 2 teaspoons lemon juice. Spread over chops. Broil till done, about 4 to 6 minutes more. Garnish with orange slices, if desired. Makes 4 servings.

FRUITED CHICKEN BREASTS

157 calories / serving

Delicate sauce blends orange juice with grapes—

    3 large chicken breasts (2 pounds),
        skinned and boned
    1 chicken bouillon cube
    ¼ teaspoon grated orange peel
    ¼ cup orange juice
    1 tablespoon chopped green onion
    1 tablespoon cornstarch
    ½ cup halved and seeded Tokay
        or seedless green grapes
      Paprika
    1 medium orange, sliced

Cut chicken breasts in half lengthwise. Sprinkle with salt; arrange chicken in 10x6x1¾-inch baking dish. Dissolve bouillon cube in ½ cup boiling water; stir in orange peel, orange juice, chopped green onion, and dash pepper. Pour over chicken. Cover with foil; bake at 350° till tender, about 50 to 60 minutes. Remove chicken to warm serving platter.

Strain pan juices, reserving ¾ cup for sauce. In saucepan blend cornstarch with 2 tablespoons cold water; stir in reserved pan juices. Cook, stirring constantly, till mixture is thick and bubbly; cook 1 minute longer.

Stir in grapes; heat through. To serve, spoon sauce over chicken; sprinkle with paprika. Garnish with orange slices. Makes 6 servings.

Broiled Chicken is a year-round favorite prepared indoors or grilled outside over the barbecue. As chicken halves cook, brush with zesty mustard-soy glaze to improve browning and flavor.

TOMATO-SAUCED CHICKEN
151 calories / serving

Oven-baked chicken takes on an Italian flavor—

Skin and bone 3 large or 6 small chicken breasts (2 pounds). Place in 11¾x7½x1¾-inch baking dish; sprinkle with 1 teaspoon seasoned salt and dash paprika. Drain one 16-ounce can tomato wedges, reserving ¼ cup liquid. Arrange tomatoes; 1 medium onion, thinly sliced and separated into rings; and one 4-ounce can sliced mushrooms, drained, over chicken.

Sprinkle 2 tablespoons snipped parsley; ½ teaspoon dried oregano leaves, crushed; and ½ teaspoon celery seed over all. Mix reserved liquid; 1 clove garlic, minced; and 1 bay leaf. Pour over chicken. Cover. Bake at 350° for 1 hour. Uncover; bake 10 minutes more. Remove bay leaf. Spoon juices over chicken. Serves 6.

LOW-CALORIE

COOKING TIP

Remove skin from poultry to reduce calories

Skinning poultry removes about 20 calories per serving. One 3½-ounce serving of light meat, skinned, provides 101 calories compared to an equal serving of dark meat, skinned, which contributes 112 calories.

BROILED CHICKEN*
271 calories / serving

Quarter chicken for smaller servings—

Blend ½ cup low-calorie Italian salad dressing, ¼ cup soy sauce, ¼ cup finely chopped onion, and 1 teaspoon dry mustard; mix well.

Halve and skin three 1½-pound ready-to-cook broiler-fryer chickens; brush with soy mixture. Place chicken in bottom of broiler pan (no rack). Broil 5 to 7 inches from heat for 20 minutes; brush occasionally. Turn. Broil till meat is tender, about 20 minutes; brush occasionally with mixture. Makes 6 servings.

*To grill: Cook chicken over *medium* coals till lightly browned, about 20 minutes; brush occasionally with mixture. Turn; broil till tender, 15 to 20 minutes; brush occasionally.

CURRIED CHICKEN
249 calories / serving

Grapefruit sections spark tomato-curry sauce—

In skillet combine ½ cup water, ½ cup vegetable juice cocktail, and 1 chicken bouillon cube, crushed. Add one 2- to 2½-pound ready-to-cook broiler-fryer chicken, cut up and skinned; ½ cup chopped onion; 1 teaspoon curry powder; ½ teaspoon poultry seasoning; ½ teaspoon salt; and dash pepper. Simmer, covered, 45 minutes. Remove chicken; skim off fat.

Blend 1 cup additional vegetable juice cocktail with 1 tablespoon all-purpose flour; add to skillet. Cook and stir till thick and bubbly. Return chicken to sauce; top with one 8½-ounce can unsweetened grapefruit sections, drained. Cover and heat through. Makes 4 servings.

VEGETABLE-COD BAKE

111 calories / serving

Fresh mushrooms highlight this main dish—

Thaw one 16-ounce package frozen cod fillets; cut into 4 portions. Place in greased 10x6x1¾-inch baking dish; sprinkle with 3 tablespoons lemon juice, 1 teaspoon salt, and ½ teaspoon paprika. Combine ½ cup sliced fresh mushrooms, ¼ cup chopped tomato, ¼ cup chopped green pepper, and 1 tablespoon snipped parsley; sprinkle over fish. Bake, covered, at 350° till fish flakes easily with fork, about 25 minutes. Serve with lemon wedges. Makes 4 servings.

FOIL-BAKED HALIBUT

139 calories / serving

Vegetable and fish cook in individual packets—

1 16-ounce package frozen halibut
   fillets, thawed
4 teaspoons lemon juice
2 carrots, cut in julienne strips
1 small green pepper, cut in rings
1 medium onion, sliced

Cut fish into 4 portions. Tear off four 1-foot lengths of heavy foil. Center fish portion on each piece of foil. Sprinkle *each* portion with ¼ teaspoon salt, dash pepper, dash paprika, and 1 teaspoon lemon juice. Divide vegetables among packets; layer atop fish. Draw up 4 corners of foil to center; twist securely. Bake at 450° till fish flakes easily with a fork, about 25 minutes. Makes 4 servings.

LEMON-HADDOCK BAKE

106 calories / serving

Sauterne adds flavor without adding calories—

Thaw two 16-ounce packages frozen haddock fillets; cut into 8 portions. Place in greased 11¾x7½x1¾-inch baking dish. Sprinkle with ½ teaspoon salt. Top with 1 cup sliced fresh mushrooms, ¼ cup chopped onion, ¼ cup chopped green pepper, and 8 thin lemon slices. Pour ¼ cup dry sauterne over all; sprinkle with paprika. Cover; bake at 350° till fish flakes, about 30 minutes. Makes 8 servings.

ITALIAN-SAUCED FISH

149 calories / serving

Canned spaghetti sauce is a time-saver—

2 16-ounce packages frozen flounder
   fillets, thawed
1 8-ounce can spaghetti sauce with
   mushrooms
2 tablespoons chopped onion
1 4-ounce package shredded mozzarella
   cheese (1 cup)

Arrange fillets in single layer on well-greased 15½x10½x1-inch baking sheet. Sprinkle with salt. Mix spaghetti sauce and onion; pour over fillets. Bake, uncovered, at 350° till fish flakes easily with fork, about 25 to 30 minutes. Sprinkle with cheese; return to oven till cheese melts, about 3 minutes. Serves 8.

ORANGE-HALIBUT FILLETS

142 calories / serving

Dill accents orange juice marinade—

1 16-ounce package frozen halibut
   fillets, thawed
2 tablespoons orange juice
   concentrate, thawed
1 tablespoon snipped parsley
1 tablespoon lemon juice
½ teaspoon dried dillweed
4 thin orange slices

Cut fish into 4 portions; place in shallow pan. Mix concentrate, next 3 ingredients, ½ cup water, and ¼ teaspoon salt; pour over fish. Marinate 30 minutes; turn once. Remove fish; reserve marinade. Place fish on well-greased broiler pan. Broil 3 inches from heat for 6 minutes. Turn; broil till fish flakes easily with fork, about 5 to 6 minutes. Baste with reserved marinade. To serve, brush with marinade; top with orange slices. Makes 4 servings.

Pizza-flavored fish entrée

Dieters who avoid calorie-laden pizza will→ welcome Italian-Sauced Fish which sports a tomato-cheese topping similar to pizza.

SALMON DOLMAS

216 calories / serving

Saucy cabbage rolls with a salmon-rice filling—

 1 beaten egg
 ¼ cup finely chopped onion
 1 teaspoon Worcestershire sauce
 1 16-ounce can pink salmon, drained,
  flaked, and bones removed
 ¾ cup cooked rice
 6 large cabbage leaves
  Cheese Sauce
  Paprika

Mix first 3 ingredients, ¼ teaspoon salt, and dash pepper. Add salmon and rice; mix well. Immerse cabbage in boiling water till limp, 2 to 3 minutes; drain. Slit heavy center vein of cabage 2 inches up leaf. Place ⅓ cup salmon mixture on each leaf; fold in sides and tuck ends under. Place in 11¾x7½x1¾-inch baking dish, seam side down. Cover with foil; bake at 350° for 45 minutes. Serve with Cheese Sauce; garnish with paprika. Makes 6 servings.

Cheese Sauce: Melt 1 tablespoon butter or margarine; blend in 4 teaspoons all-purpose flour, ¼ teaspoon salt, and dash pepper. Add 1 cup skim milk; cook and stir till thick and bubbly. Remove sauce from heat; add 2 ounces process Swiss cheese, shredded (½ cup), and 1 tablespoon lemon juice. Stir till cheese melts.

SWEET AND SOUR SHRIMP

187 calories / serving

Chow mein noodles add crunch to this main dish—

Drain one 15¼-ounce can pineapple chunks (juice pack); reserve juice. Add water to juice to make 1⅛ cups. Cut up pineapple, if desired.

In saucepan combine juice mixture; pineapple; 1 medium green pepper, cut in strips; ¼ cup sliced green onion with tops; and 1 vegetable bouillon cube. Heat to boiling; simmer, covered, 3 to 4 minutes. Blend 2 tablespoons brown sugar, 4 teaspoons cornstarch, 1 tablespoon cold water, and 2 teaspoons vinegar. Add to pineapple mixture. Cook and stir till thick and bubbly. Fold in two 4½-ounce cans shrimp, drained and deveined. Heat through.

Serve over one 3-ounce can chow mein noodles (2¼ cups), warmed. Makes 6 servings.

LOW-CALORIE

COOKING TIP

Make white sauce with little or no fat

Blend flour with a small amount of cold skim milk. Stir into remaining milk and fat (if used). Cook and stir till bubbly. For rich color, add a few drops yellow food coloring.

SEAFOOD DIVAN

115 calories / serving

An elegant casserole for entertaining—

Cook two 10-ounce packages frozen broccoli spears following package directions; drain. Arrange in greased 11¾x7½x1¾-inch baking dish. Toss one 5-ounce can lobster, drained and flaked, with one 4½-ounce can shrimp, drained and deveined; spoon over broccoli.

In shaker combine ¼ cup skim milk, 2 tablespoons all-purpose flour, and ¼ teaspoon salt; shake well. Combine flour mixture, 1¼ cups skim milk, and 1 tablespoon butter. Cook and stir till thick and bubbly; reduce heat. Add 2 ounces process Swiss cheese, shredded (½ cup); stir to melt. Pour over seafood, completely covering seafood; sprinkle with paprika. Bake at 400° till hot, 20 to 25 minutes. Serves 8.

BASIC MEAT LOAF

271 calories / serving

Juicy, flavorful loaf topped with chili sauce—

 1 beef bouillon cube
 1 beaten egg
 1½ cups soft bread crumbs
 ¼ cup chopped onion
 ½ teaspoon ground sage
 1 pound lean ground beef
 3 tablespoons chili sauce

Dissolve bouillon cube in ¼ cup boiling water. Mix bouillon with egg, crumbs, onion, sage, ¼ teaspoon salt, and dash pepper. Add beef; mix well. Shape into loaf in shallow baking dish. Bake at 350° for 45 minutes. Spread chili sauce over loaf. Bake 10 to 15 minutes more. Serves 4.

CRANBERRY-SAUCED BURGERS

235 calories / serving

Colorful sauce complements broiled beef patties—

- 1 pound lean ground beef
- 1 tablespoon finely chopped onion
- 1 tablespoon cornstarch
- 1 tablespoon sugar
- ¾ cup low-calorie cranberry juice cocktail
- 2 teaspoons lemon juice

Combine beef, onion, ½ teaspoon salt, and dash pepper; shape into 4 patties, ¾ inch thick. Broil 3 inches from heat for 6 minutes; turn. Broil till done, about 4 minutes. In saucepan combine cornstarch, sugar, and dash salt. Gradually add cranberry juice. Cook and stir till thick and bubbly. Stir in lemon juice. Pass cranberry sauce with burgers. Makes 4 servings.

TURKEY HAWAIIAN

310 calories / serving

An excellent way to use leftover turkey—

- 1 15¼-ounce can pineapple slices (juice pack)
- 1 10½-ounce can condensed chicken broth
- 1 10-ounce package frozen peas
- 1 2-ounce can sliced mushrooms, drained
- 1½ cups bias-cut celery slices
- ¼ cup chopped onion
- ¼ cup soy sauce
- 3 tablespoons cornstarch
- 3 cups diced, cooked turkey
- 1 5-ounce can water chestnuts, drained and sliced
- 4 cups cooked rice

Drain pineapple, reserving juice; add water to juice to make 1 cup. In large saucepan combine juice mixture, broth, peas, mushrooms, celery, onion, and soy sauce; bring to boiling. Cover; simmer for 5 minutes. Blend cornstarch with 3 tablespoons cold water; add to saucepan. Cook and stir till thickened and bubbly.

Cut up pineapple. Stir pineapple, turkey, and water chestnuts into saucepan; heat through. Serve over hot cooked rice. Serves 8.

STUFFED PEPPERS

212 calories / serving

A calorie-trimmed version of a favorite dish—

Cut off tops of 8 medium green peppers; remove seeds and membrane. Precook peppers in boiling, salted water for 5 minutes; drain. (For crisper peppers, omit precooking.) Generously sprinkle inside of peppers with salt.

In skillet brown 1 pound lean ground beef with ¼ cup chopped onion; drain. Stir in 1½ cups croutons; 2 ounces mozzarella cheese, shredded (½ cup); one 2-ounce can chopped mushrooms, drained; 2 medium tomatoes, coarsely chopped; ½ teaspoon Worcestershire sauce; and ½ teaspoon salt. Spoon into peppers.

Place in 10x6x1¾-inch baking dish. Bake, covered, at 350° for 25 minutes. Uncover; sprinkle with 2 ounces mozzarella cheese, shredded (½ cup). Bake 5 to 10 minutes more. Serves 8.

FRANK-KRAUT SKILLET

211 calories / serving

Caraway seed enhances this jiffy entrée—

- 4 frankfurters
- 1 16-ounce can sauerkraut
- ½ teaspoon caraway seed
- 2 ounces process Swiss cheese, shredded (½ cup)

Slice franks diagonally into ½-inch pieces; brown in skillet. Add undrained sauerkraut and caraway seed. Cook and stir over medium heat till most of liquid is gone. Stir in cheese; heat till melted, 2 to 3 minutes. Serves 4.

WIENER-KRAUT BAKE

212 calories / serving

A popular duo baked in vegetable juice cocktail—

In 1½-quart casserole combine one 16-ounce can sauerkraut, drained and chopped; ¾ cup vegetable juice cocktail; 1 tablespoon chopped onion; and 1 tablespoon prepared mustard.

Arrange 4 frankfurters atop kraut mixture. Bake, covered, at 350° for 50 minutes. Top with 1 medium green pepper, cut in thin rings. Bake, covered, 10 minutes more. Makes 4 servings.

PUFFY OMELET

103 calories / serving

An impressive dish requiring few ingredients—

- 4 egg whites
- 2 tablespoons water
- ¼ teaspoon salt
- 4 egg yolks
- 1 tablespoon butter or margarine

Beat egg whites till frothy; add water and salt. Beat till stiff peaks form. Beat egg yolks till thick and lemon-colored. Fold yolks into whites. Melt butter in 10-inch ovenproof skillet; heat till drop of water sizzles.

Pour in omelet mixture; spread to edges of skillet, leaving sides higher. Reduce heat; cook till puffed and bottom is golden, 8 minutes. Bake at 325° till knife inserted in center comes out clean, 8 to 10 minutes.

Loosen sides of omelet. Make shallow, off-center cut across omelet. Tilt pan; fold smaller portion over larger portion. Slip onto platter. Serve immediately. Makes 4 servings.

MACARONI-CHEESE PUFF

226 calories / serving

As pictured opposite contents page—

- ½ cup small elbow macaroni
- 1½ cups skim milk
- 6 ounces sharp process American cheese, shredded (1½ cups)
- 3 beaten egg yolks
- 1 cup soft bread crumbs (1½ slices)
- ¼ cup chopped canned pimiento
- 2 tablespoons chopped green onion
- 3 egg whites
- ¼ teaspoon cream of tartar

Cook macaroni in boiling, salted water till tender; drain. Combine milk, cheese, and ¼ teaspoon salt; stir over low heat till cheese melts. Stir small amount of hot mixture into egg yolks. Return to hot mixture; blend well.

Stir in macaroni, crumbs, pimiento, and onion. Beat egg whites with cream of tartar till stiff. Fold into macaroni mixture. Pour into *ungreased* 1½-quart soufflé dish. Bake at 325° till knife inserted off-center comes out clean, about 1 hour. Serve immediately. Serves 6.

LOW-CALORIE

COOKING TIP

Cook eggs in little or no fat in nonstick pan

Before cooking omelet, lightly brush nonstick skillet with salad oil. Pour omelet mixture into skillet and cook. Using spatula, mark omelet in thirds with two shallow parallel cuts.

To remove omelet from skillet, tilt skillet. Gently fold each side of omelet over center portion, envelope-style. Carefully slip folded omelet onto warm serving platter.

SWISS CHEESE SOUFFLÉ
273 calories / serving

A tempting main dish for lunch or brunch—

In saucepan melt 2 tablespoons butter; blend in 3 tablespoons all-purpose flour, ½ teaspoon salt, and dash cayenne. Add 1 cup skim milk; cook and stir till thick and bubbly. Remove from heat. Add 4 ounces process Swiss cheese, shredded (1 cup); stir till cheese melts.

Beat 4 egg yolks till thick and lemon-colored. Add cheese mixture, stirring constantly; cool slightly. Beat 4 egg whites to stiff peaks. Pour yolk mixture over whites; fold together thoroughly. Pour into *ungreased* 5-cup soufflé dish. For a top hat that puffs in the oven, trace a circle through mixture 1 inch from edge and 1 inch deep. Bake at 300° till knife inserted off-center comes out clean, about 1¼ hours. Serve immediately. Makes 4 servings.

MUSHROOM OMELET
123 calories / serving

Vary the filling to suit family tastes—

With fork beat 3 eggs, 1 tablespoon water, ¼ teaspoon salt, dash pepper, and dash mixed salad herbs till blended but not frothy. Lightly brush 8-inch skillet with salad oil; heat.

Add eggs; cook slowly. Run spatula around edges; lift to allow uncooked portion to flow underneath. Cook till set but still shiny. Remove from heat; spoon one 2-ounce can sliced mushrooms, heated and drained, down center of omelet. With spatula, fold omelet, envelope-style. Tilt pan; slip onto platter. Serves 2.

TOMATO-EGG SCRAMBLE
136 calories / serving

Quick fix-up for a late-night supper—

With fork beat together 6 eggs; ¼ cup skim milk; ½ teaspoon salt; ¼ teaspoon dried oregano leaves, crushed; ¼ teaspoon dried parsley flakes; and dash pepper. Pour into warm nonstick skillet. Cook over low heat; with spatula lift mixture from bottom of pan. When half done, fold in one 8-ounce can tomatoes, drained and cut up. Serve immediately. Serves 4.

SHRIMP-MUSHROOM SOUFFLÉ
202 calories / serving

Another time substitute crab for the shrimp—

- 2 tablespoons butter or margarine
- 3 tablespoons all-purpose flour
- ½ teaspoon salt
- 1 cup skim milk
- 4 egg yolks
- 1 4½-ounce can shrimp, drained, deveined, and finely chopped
- 1 2-ounce can mushrooms, drained and finely chopped
- 2 tablespoons snipped parsley
- 4 egg whites

In saucepan melt butter; blend in flour, salt, and dash pepper. Add milk; cook and stir till thick and bubbly. Remove from heat.

Beat egg yolks till thick and lemon-colored. Slowly add white sauce, stirring constantly. Stir in shrimp, mushrooms, and parsley.

Beat egg whites to stiff peaks. Gradually pour shrimp mixture over egg whites, folding together thoroughly. Turn into *ungreased* 5-cup soufflé dish. Bake at 325° till knife inserted off-center comes out clean, about 60 minutes. Serve immediately. Makes 4 servings.

Tomatoes and herbs add flavor to eggs in Tomato-Egg Scramble. For variety, add sliced mushrooms or green pepper strips.

CALORIE-LEAN VEGETABLES

CAULIFLOWER ITALIANO
35 calories / serving

Colorful in appearance as well as flavor—

- 1 tablespoon chopped onion
- 1 small clove garlic, crushed
- 2 tablespoons low-calorie Italian salad dressing
- 3 cups small fresh cauliflowerets
- 2 tablespoons chopped green pepper
- 1 cup cherry tomatoes, halved
- ½ teaspoon salt
- ⅛ teaspoon dried basil leaves, crushed

In 8-inch skillet cook onion and garlic in salad dressing till tender; add cauliflowerets and ¼ cup water. Cook, covered, over low heat for 10 minutes. Add green pepper; cook till cauliflower is tender, about 5 minutes. Stir in remaining ingredients; heat through. Serves 6.

ASPARAGUS WITH CHEESE
78 calories / serving

Sesame seed, cheese, and pimiento top spears—

- 1 pound fresh asparagus spears *or* one 10-ounce package frozen asparagus spears
- 2 ounces process Swiss cheese, shredded (½ cup)
- 2 tablespoons chopped canned pimiento
- 2 teaspoons sesame seed, toasted

In 10-inch skillet cook asparagus spears in boiling, salted water till tender; drain. Toss together cheese, pimiento, and sesame seed; sprinkle over spears. Heat at 350° just till cheese melts, about 3 minutes. Makes 4 servings.

Unlimited vegetables

←Enticing vegetable dishes, such as Cauliflower Italiano and Asparagus with Cheese, offer low-calorie eating at its best.

RUBY-SAUCED BEETS
61 calories / serving

A delicate blend of cranberry and orange—

In saucepan blend 2 teaspoons cornstarch, 2 teaspoons sugar, and dash salt. Stir in ½ cup low-calorie cranberry juice cocktail; stir over medium heat till thickened and bubbly. Add one 16-ounce can sliced beets, drained, and ¼ teaspoon shredded orange peel. Simmer, uncovered, for 10 minutes. Makes 4 servings.

ORIENTAL SPINACH
25 calories / serving

To enhance vegetable flavor, serve piping hot—

Cook one 10-ounce package frozen chopped spinach following package directions; do not drain. Stir in one 16-ounce can bean sprouts, drained and rinsed; and one 5-ounce can water chestnuts, drained and sliced. Heat to boiling; drain. Toss with 4 teaspoons soy sauce. Serves 8.

BASIL CARROTS
39 calories / serving

A good Sunday dinner vegetable—

Slice 6 medium carrots. Simmer, covered, in salted water till tender, about 10 to 15 minutes; drain. Combine 1 tablespoon melted butter; ¼ teaspoon salt; and ¼ teaspoon dried basil leaves, crushed; toss with carrots. Serves 6.

TURNIP-CARROT DUO
35 calories / serving

Excellent pot roast accompaniment—

Cover and cook 1½ cups cubed, peeled turnips and 1½ cups sliced carrots in boiling, salted water till tender, about 15 minutes; drain. Add 1 tablespoon snipped parsley, 2 teaspoons butter, and 1 teaspoon lemon juice; toss. Serves 6.

BROCCOLI-TOMATO STACK-UPS

68 calories/serving

A quick and colorful vegetable duo—

Prepare one 10-ounce package frozen chopped broccoli according to package directions; drain. Cut 3 large tomatoes into 4 slices each. Sprinkle tomato slices with salt; place on baking sheet. Shred 2 ounces process Swiss cheese (½ cup). Combine broccoli, *2 tablespoons* of the cheese, and 2 tablespoons chopped onion. Spoon broccoli mixture atop tomato slices. Broil 4 to 5 inches from heat till hot, about 10 to 12 minutes. Sprinkle with remaining cheese. Return tomatoes to broiler till cheese melts, about 1 to 2 minutes. Makes 6 servings.

HERBED TOMATO HALVES

56 calories/serving

Crisp topping has a subtle herb flavor—

      3 medium tomatoes, cut in half
         crosswise
      ⅛ cup soft bread crumbs
      1 tablespoon butter, melted
      ¼ teaspoon dried basil leaves, crushed
      2 tablespoons grated Parmesan cheese

Arrange tomato halves in 10x6x1¾-inch baking dish. Sprinkle with salt. Toss bread crumbs with melted butter, basil, and cheese. Sprinkle on tomato halves. Bake, uncovered, at 350° for 20 to 25 minutes. Makes 6 servings.

SEASONING GUIDE FOR VEGETABLES

Spices and herbs add appeal without adding calories. Add seasoning to vegetable as it cooks or lightly sprinkle over food before serving. Begin with ¼ teaspoon dried herb for each 4 servings and increase until desired flavor level is reached. To use dried herbs in leaf form, measure and then crush before adding to vegetable. To use fresh herbs, use 3 times more of the seasoning and snip, rather than crush. Use fresh herbs when available.

Artichoke	bay leaf, marjoram, thyme
Asparagus	caraway seed, mustard, nutmeg, sesame seed, tarragon
Beans—green	basil, dill, marjoram, mustard, nutmeg, oregano, savory, thyme
Beets	allspice, bay leaf, caraway seed, cloves, ginger, mustard
Broccoli	caraway seed, mustard, oregano, tarragon
Brussels sprouts	caraway seed, mustard, nutmeg, sage
Cabbage	caraway seed, celery seed, cumin, curry powder, fennel, mustard
Carrots	allspice, bay leaf, cinnamon, curry powder, dill, ginger
Cauliflower	cayenne, celery seed, chili powder, nutmeg, paprika, rosemary
Corn	cayenne, celery seed, chili powder, curry powder, paprika
Eggplant	allspice, bay leaf, chili powder, marjoram
Onions	bay leaf, mustard, oregano, paprika, sage
Peas	chili powder, dill, oregano, poppy seed, rosemary, sage
Potatoes	caraway seed, fennel, mustard, oregano, paprika, sesame seed
Spinach	allspice, cinnamon, nutmeg, oregano, rosemary, sesame seed
Squash	allspice, bay leaf, cinnamon, cloves, ginger, nutmeg, paprika
Sweet potatoes	cardamom seed, cinnamon, cloves, nutmeg, poppy seed
Tomatoes	basil, celery seed, chili powder, curry powder, oregano
Turnips	allspice, celery seed, curry powder, dill, oregano

Keep vegetable dishes low in calories

COOKING TIP

Substitute lemon juice or crushed herbs for butter or margarine to add flavor to vegetables and to keep calorie count at a minimum.

BAKED DEVILED TOMATOES

51 calories/serving

Festive vegetable combo bakes atop tomatoes—

4 large tomatoes, halved
Salt
1 tablespoon prepared mustard
. . .
2 tablespoons chopped green pepper
2 tablespoons chopped celery
1 tablespoon chopped green onion
2 tablespoons butter or margarine, melted

Place tomatoes, cut side up, in baking dish. Sprinkle with salt. Spread cut side of tomatoes with mustard. Combine green pepper, celery, onion, and melted butter or margarine; spoon mixture over tomatoes. Bake at 425° for 8 to 10 minutes. Makes 8 servings.

SKILLET SQUASH

50 calories/serving

Each vegetable flavor complements the others—

Scrub 2 medium zucchini squash in water; cut off ends. Cut into thin crosswise slices (about 2 cups). Thinly slice 1 medium onion; separate into rings (about 1½ cups). In 12-inch skillet melt 2 teaspoons butter; add ½ teaspoon salt and dash coarsely ground pepper. Cook onion in butter till crisp-tender. Add squash. Cook, covered, for 6 minutes, stirring occasionally. Add 1 medium tomato, cut in wedges, and one 2-ounce can sliced mushrooms, drained. Continue cooking, covered, till tomato and mushrooms are hot and squash is crisp-tender, about 4 minutes. Remove vegetables to serving bowl with slotted spoon. Makes 6 servings.

CABBAGE SCRAMBLE

45 calories/serving

Vegetable bouillon blends flavors together—

In 8-inch skillet combine ½ cup water; 2 vegetable bouillon cubes, crushed; and ¼ teaspoon dried oregano leaves, crushed (optional). Shred ½ small head cabbage (3 cups) and 3 medium carrots (1 cup). Thinly slice 1 medium onion (½ cup). Add vegetables to skillet mixture. Cook, covered, over low heat, till vegetables are tender, about 15 to 20 minutes; stir occasionally. Drain before serving. Makes 4 servings.

SAUCY BRUSSELS SPROUTS

62 calories/serving

Delicate cheese sauce tops sprouts—

Thaw two 8-ounce packages frozen Brussels sprouts enough to separate; halve larger sprouts. Cook following package directions; do not drain. Add one 5-ounce can water chestnuts, drained and sliced; heat through. Blend one 3-ounce package Neufchatel cheese, softened, and ¼ cup skim milk. Add ½ teaspoon prepared mustard, 1 teaspoon lemon juice, and dash salt; beat well. Stir over low heat till hot. Drain sprouts; pour sauce over. Serves 8.

Team zucchini squash with tomato wedges, onion rings, and sliced mushrooms for a colorful vegetable idea—Skillet Squash.

Low-calorie Sesame Broccoli, topped with toasted sesame seeds and coated with soy mixture, is sure to become a family favorite.

SESAME BROCCOLI
74 calories / serving

Good with roast beef or chicken dinner—

Cook 1 pound fresh broccoli in small amount of boiling, salted water till tender, about 15 minutes; drain. In saucepan combine 1 tablespoon salad oil; 1 tablespoon vinegar; 1 tablespoon soy sauce; 4 teaspoons sugar; and 1 tablespoon sesame seed, toasted. Heat to boiling. Pour over broccoli; turn spears to coat. Serves 5.

PEAS WITH MUSHROOMS
38 calories / serving

Flavored with lemon juice and basil—

Cook one 10-ounce package frozen peas according to package directions; do not drain. Add one 6-ounce can sliced mushrooms, drained; heat through. Drain. Add 1 teaspoon lemon juice and ¼ teaspoon dried basil leaves, crushed. Season with salt and pepper. Makes 6 servings.

VEGETABLE FIESTA
62 calories / serving

A colorful and appealing vegetable combo—

    1 16-ounce can tomato wedges, drained
    1 12-ounce can whole kernel corn
    1 medium green pepper, coarsely
         chopped
    ¼ teaspoon celery seed
       Dash ground oregano

In saucepan combine all ingredients, 1½ teaspoons salt, and dash pepper. Cook, uncovered, over medium heat till green pepper is tender, 8 to 10 minutes. Stir occasionally. Serves 6.

CORN MEDLEY
50 calories / serving

Chicken bouillon adds a satisfying flavor—

    1 10-ounce package frozen whole
         kernel corn
    ½ cup chopped celery
    1 chicken bouillon cube, crushed
    1 2-ounce can sliced mushrooms,
         drained
    1 medium tomato, cut in thin wedges

In saucepan combine corn, celery, bouillon cube, and ⅓ cup water. Bring to boiling; cover and simmer till vegetables are tender, about 5 to 7 minutes. Stir in mushrooms and tomato wedges; heat through. Season to taste with salt and pepper. Makes 6 servings.

BAKED-STUFFED POTATOES
60 calories / serving

As pictured on the cover—

Scrub 3 medium baking potatoes; puncture skin with fork. Bake at 425° for 1 hour. Cut potatoes in half lengthwise. Scoop out inside; mash. Combine ⅓ cup hot water, 3 tablespoons nonfat dry milk powder, ½ teaspoon salt *or* imitation butter-flavored salt, and dash pepper. Add to potatoes; beat till fluffy, adding additional hot water if needed. Pile lightly into shells; sprinkle with paprika. Return to oven till hot, about 10 minutes. Makes 6 servings.

LOW-CALORIE

COOKING TIP

Vegetable cooking methods should add flavor, not calories

Waterless cooking allows fresh vegetables to cook in their own natural juices. Vegetables are cooked over low to medium heat with little or no liquid added. Seasonings may be added to vegetables before or after cooking.

SKILLET ONION SLICES
42 calories / serving

Makes a good steak or liver accompaniment—

- ¼ cup low-calorie Italian salad dressing
- 3 large onions, cut in ½-inch slices
- 2 tablespoons snipped parsley
- 2 tablespoons shredded Parmesan cheese Paprika

In skillet heat salad dressing, ⅓ cup water, and ½ teaspoon salt. Place onion slices in single layer in skillet. Cover; cook over low heat, 10 minutes. Turn; sprinkle with parsley, cheese, and paprika. Cook, covered, 5 minutes; cook, uncovered, 5 minutes more. Serves 6.

GREEN BEANS WITH ONIONS
61 calories / serving

Easy to make for unexpected company—

- 1 9-ounce package frozen cut green beans
- ½ teaspoon dried marjoram leaves, crushed
- 1 8-ounce can peeled, small, whole, stewed onions, drained
- 1 tablespoon butter or margarine

Cook beans according to package directions, *except add marjoram to cooking liquid.* Halve onions lengthwise; add to beans during last few minutes of cooking time. Continue cooking till onions are heated through. Drain thoroughly; stir in butter or margarine. Turn vegetables into serving dish. Makes 4 servings.

ONION-POTATO BAKE
87 calories / serving

An excellent oven-meal vegetable—

- 2 medium baking potatoes, peeled and thinly sliced (2½ cups)
- 3 medium onions, thinly sliced Salt Pepper
- ½ cup skim milk
- 2 tablespoons chopped pimiento
- 2 tablespoons snipped parsley
- 2 ounces process Swiss cheese, shredded (½ cup)

Layer *half* the potatoes and *half* the onions in greased 10x6x1¾-inch baking dish. Sprinkle generously with salt and pepper. Combine milk, pimiento, and parsley; pour *half* the mixture over onion-potato layer. Repeat layers.

Cover; bake at 350° till vegetables are tender, about 60 to 65 minutes. Uncover. Sprinkle shredded cheese over top; return to oven till cheese melts. Makes 6 servings.

Sprinkle gala green beans and stewed onions with a touch of marjoram for a delectable combination in Green Beans with Onions.

SALADS FOR THE CALORIE COUNTER

CHICKEN-ROMAINE SALAD

121 calories / serving

Crisp croutons give salad crunchy texture—

- 1 head romaine, torn in bite-size pieces (8 cups)
- 2 cups cubed cooked chicken
- 2 tablespoons grated Parmesan cheese
- ⅔ cup low-calorie Italian salad dressing
- 4 teaspoons tarragon vinegar
- ½ teaspoon dry mustard
- ¼ teaspoon Worcestershire sauce
- 1 cup croutons

Combine romaine, chicken, and Parmesan. Mix salad dressing and next 3 indredients. Toss *half* of the mixture with croutons; don't soak. Add to salad with remaining dressing. Serves 6.

PEACH AND CHICKEN CUPS

220 calories / serving

Green pepper rings hold each serving—

- 2 medium chicken breasts, skinned, boned, cooked, and chilled (1 pound)
- 1 3-ounce package Neufchatel cheese, softened
- ¼ cup low-calorie mayonnaise-type dressing
- ¼ teaspoon dried thyme leaves, crushed
- ⅛ teaspoon dried basil leaves, crushed
- 1 16-ounce can peach halves (juice pack), drained and diced
- ½ cup chopped celery
- 1 green pepper, sliced in 4 thick rings
- Lettuce leaves

Cube chicken. Mix cheese, next 3 ingredients, dash salt, and dash pepper. Add chicken, peaches, and celery; toss. Chill. Spoon mixture into pepper rings; serve on lettuce. Serves 4.

CHICKEN-ARTICHOKE BOWL

245 calories / serving

Flavorful artichoke marinade becomes the salad dressing at serving time—

- ¾ cup low-calorie Russian salad dressing
- 2 tablespoons water
- 4 thin slices onion, separated into rings
- 1 clove garlic, crushed
- ¼ teaspoon celery seed
- ½ teaspoon salt
  Dash pepper
- 1 9-ounce package frozen artichoke hearts
- 1 2-ounce jar pimientos, drained and chopped (¼ cup)

  • • •

- 3 large chicken breasts, skinned, boned, cooked, and chilled (about 2 pounds)

  • • •

- 2 cups *each* torn lettuce, torn romaine, and torn fresh spinach

In medium saucepan combine salad dressing, water, onion, garlic, celery seed, salt, and pepper. Bring to boiling; add frozen artichoke hearts. Cook hearts till tender, about 3 to 5 minutes. Stir in chopped pimiento; chill. Cut chilled chicken into cubes.

At serving time drain chilled artichoke mixture, reserving marinade. Cut artichokes into bite-sized pieces, if desired. Toss artichoke mixture with chicken cubes, torn greens, and enough of the reserved marinade to coat greens; toss lightly. Makes 6 servings.

Main dish salad bowl

Center a tomato rose atop Chicken-Romaine Salad. Sharp Romaine flavor mingles with chicken, grated cheese, and croutons.

Toss succulent Super Chef Salad in a big bowl at the table. Bread sticks and a beverage are all you need to complete the meal.

COTTAGE-SHRIMP TOSS

165 calories / serving

Toss cottage cheese with the salad—

    6 cups torn Boston or bibb lettuce
    1 tablespoon salad oil
    1 tablespoon wine vinegar
          . . .
    2 7-ounce packages frozen shrimp in
        shells, cooked, peeled, and cleaned
    1 12-ounce carton cream-style cottage
        cheese (1½ cups)
    ¼ cup coarsely chopped dill pickle
    2 tablespoons sliced green onion

In bowl sprinkle lettuce with salt and pepper; toss with oil and vinegar. Reserve a few whole shrimp; coarsely chop remaining shrimp. Toss chopped shrimp and remaining ingredients with lettuce. Garnish with whole shrimp. Serves 6.

SUPER CHEF SALAD

154 calories / serving

Dressing is French-Italian combination—

In large salad bowl arrange 6 cups torn lettuce; 2 tomatoes, cut in wedges; 3 hard-cooked eggs, cut in wedges; 1 small onion, sliced and separated into rings; 4 ounces fully cooked ham, cut in thin strips; and 4 ounces sharp natural Cheddar cheese, cut in strips. Combine ¼ cup low-calorie Italian salad dressing and ¼ cup low-calorie French-style salad dressing; pour over salad. Toss. Makes 8 servings.

CURRIED SHRIMP SALAD

119 calories / serving

Use canned shrimp to cut the preparation time—

Drain two 4½-ounce cans shrimp; sprinkle shrimp with 2 tablespoons lemon juice. Add 1 cup sliced celery and 2 tablespoons snipped parsley. Stir ½ teaspoon curry powder into ½ cup low-calorie mayonnaise-type dressing; add to shrimp mixture. Chill. Just before serving toss shrimp mixture with 4 cups torn lettuce; fold in 3 hard-cooked eggs, chilled and sliced. Season with salt and pepper. Makes 6 servings.

HAM AND CHEESE MEDLEY

246 calories / serving

Pass creamy blender cottage cheese dressing—

In large bowl combine one 8½-ounce can pineapple tidbits, drained; 4 ounces fully cooked ham, cubed (1 cup); 1 cup halved and seeded grapes; and 2 ounces mozzarella cheese, cut in julienne strips (½ cup). Chill. In blender combine 1 cup dry cottage cheese, ½ cup skim milk, and ½ teaspoon paprika. Blend till smooth, about 20 seconds; chill. To serve, toss 4 cups torn lettuce with ham mixture. Serve in individual bowls. Pass dressing. Serves 4.

SCALLOP TOSS

178 calories / serving

Serve with melba toast for a bridge luncheon—

Cook one 12-ounce package frozen scallops, thawed, over low heat in small amount boiling, salted water for 3 minutes; drain and chill. Rub salad bowl with 1 clove garlic, halved; discard. In bowl arrange 2 cups *each* torn lettuce, torn romaine, and torn spinach; 3 hard-cooked eggs, quartered; ½ cup diced celery; 4 ounces mozzarella cheese, cut in thin strips; and scallops. Pour ⅓ cup low-calorie Russian salad dressing over; toss to coat. Makes 6 servings.

LOW-CALORIE

COOKING TIP

Make tomato cups to hold salad mixtures. Cut top off tomato and scoop out pulp with spoon. Turn tomatoes, cut side down, on absorbent paper toweling to drain before stuffing. Chop pulp and use in salad.

TUNA-FRUIT SALAD

150 calories / serving

Mound attractively in lettuce-lined bowls—

Toss together 2 medium unpeeled apples, cut in ½-inch cubes; 4 cups torn lettuce; one 9¼-ounce can water-pack tuna, drained and flaked; and 1 cup seedless green grapes. Cover and chill. Combine ⅔ cup low-calorie mayonnaise-type dressing, 1 tablespoon lemon juice, and ¼ teaspoon salt; toss with tuna mixture. Serves 6.

DIETER'S TUNA SALAD

78 calories / serving

Tart wine vinegar dressing enhances salad flavor

 ¾ cup wine vinegar
 2 teaspoons sugar
 1½ teaspoons dried basil leaves, crushed
 • • •
 8 cups torn lettuce
 2 6½- or 7-ounce cans water-pack tuna, drained and flaked
 1½ cups cherry tomatoes, halved
 ½ medium onion, thinly sliced and separated into rings
 1 medium cucumber, sliced
 ½ cup sliced celery

Mix first 3 ingredients and dash pepper. Chill. Toss lettuce with remaining ingredients. Add dressing; toss lightly. Serves 8.

SHRIMP-STUFFED TOMATOES

107 calories / serving

A hot salad seasoned with garlic salt—

 6 large tomatoes
 1 teaspoon garlic salt
 • • •
 ¼ cup chopped onion
 ¼ cup chopped celery
 2 tablespoons chopped green pepper
 Dash pepper
 2 4½-ounce cans shrimp, drained and chopped (2 cups)
 ½ cup croutons

Cut tops off tomatoes; scoop out pulp. Chop tops and pulp; drain well. Sprinkle inside of tomatoes with garlic salt.

In medium skillet combine tomato pulp, onion, celery, green pepper, and pepper. Simmer, covered, till vegetables are tender, about 10 to 15 minutes. Stir in shrimp and croutons. Pile shrimp mixture in tomato shells. Place in 10x6x1¾-inch baking dish; pour water into dish ½ inch deep. Bake at 375° for 20 to 25 minutes. Trim with parsley, if desired. Serves 6.

Even non-dieters can't resist crisp and colorful Dieter's Tuna Salad served with big tumblers of iced tea on a hot summer day.

Combine calorie counting with entertaining and serve Crab-Tomato Aspic fairly bursting with delicate crab meat and crisp celery.

SALMON-STUFFED TOMATOES

191 calories / serving

Gala tomato cups filled with salmon salad are perfect for entertaining at lunch—

> 1 16-ounce can pink salmon, drained
> 1 cup cream-style cottage cheese, drained
> ¼ cup low-calorie Thousand Island salad dressing
> ½ cup chopped celery
> 2 tablespoons chopped green pepper
> ¼ teaspoon onion salt
>   Dash pepper
>   • • •
> 6 medium tomatoes, chilled
>   Lettuce
> 6 lemon wedges

In medium bowl flake salmon, removing bones and skin. Add cottage cheese, low-calorie Thousand Island salad dressing, celery, green pepper, onion salt, and pepper. Mix well; chill.

With stem end down, cut each tomato into 6 wedges, *cutting to, but not through,* base of tomato. Spread wedges apart slightly; sprinkle lightly with salt. Spoon about ½ cup salmon mixture into each tomato. Serve stuffed tomatoes on lettuce-lined plates. Garnish with lemon wedges. Makes 6 servings.

CRAB-TOMATO ASPIC

125 calories / serving

An unusual main-dish tomato aspic—

Soften 2 envelopes unflavored gelatin (2 tablespoons) in ½ cup cold condensed beef broth. Combine 3 cups tomato juice, 2 slices onion, 2 bay leaves, and ¼ teaspoon celery salt; bring to boiling. Remove onion and bay leaves. Add softened gelatin; stir till dissolved. Add additional ½ cup condensed beef broth and 2 tablespoons lemon juice. Chill till partially set.

Fold in 1 cup chopped celery and one 7½-ounce can crab meat, drained, flaked, and cartilage removed. Turn into 5½-cup mold; chill till firm. Unmold; garnish with 3 hard-cooked eggs, cut in wedges. Serves 6.

CRAB-ARTICHOKE TOSS

122 calories / serving

Lower in calories than it looks—

Cook one 8-ounce package frozen artichoke hearts following package directions; drain and chill. Halve hearts. Toss with 5 cups torn lettuce; 1 tomato, cut in wedges; one 7½-ounce can crab meat, chilled, drained, cartilage removed and broken in pieces; 2 ounces process Swiss cheese, cut in strips; ¼ cup shredded carrot; 2 tablespoons sliced green onion; and ¼ cup low-calorie Italian salad dressing. Serves 6.

TANGY SEAFOOD TOSS

212 calories / serving

Red dressing is flavored with grapefruit juice—

Mix 1 tablespoon cornstarch, 1 tablespoon sugar, ½ teaspoon paprika, ½ teaspoon dry mustard, ¼ teaspoon salt, and ⅛ teaspoon pepper. Drain one 16-ounce can unsweetened grapefruit sections; reserve liquid. Blend reserved liquid into cornstarch mixture. Cook and stir till thick and bubbly. Remove from heat; stir in ¼ cup catsup and 2 tablespoons salad oil. Chill.

In bowl arrange 4 cups torn lettuce, one 7-ounce can water-pack tuna, drained and broken into chunks; ½ small cucumber, sliced; ⅓ cup sliced radishes; and grapefruit. Chill. Serve with dressing. Makes 4 servings.

SUNSHINE ASPIC

65 calories / serving

Colorful egg slices peek through aspic ring—

- 1½ cups tomato juice
- 1 bay leaf
- ¼ teaspoon celery salt
- ¼ teaspoon onion salt
- 1 envelope unflavored gelatin
  (1 tablespoon)
- ½ cup water
- 2 tablespoons lemon juice
- 2 hard-cooked eggs, sliced

Combine *1 cup* of the tomato juice with bay leaf, celery salt, and onion salt; simmer, uncovered, 5 minutes. Remove and discard bay leaf.

Meanwhile, soften gelatin in remaining cold tomato juice; add to hot juice mixture. Stir to dissolve gelatin. Stir in water and lemon juice. Chill till mixture is partially set.

Pour *half* of the chilled mixture into 3½-cup ring mold. Press egg slices gently into gelatin along outer edge of mold. Carefully pour remaining gelatin around and over egg slices. Chill till firm. Unmold. Makes 4 servings.

ORANGE PERFECTION SALAD

48 calories / serving

Crown with lettuce and orange twists—

- 1 envelope unflavored gelatin
  (1 tablespoon)
- 2 tablespoons sugar
- ¼ teaspoon salt
- ½ cup orange juice
- 1 tablespoon lemon juice
- 1 tablespoon vinegar
- 2 drops yellow food coloring

  • • •

- 1 medium orange, sectioned and diced
- 1 cup chopped cabbage
- ¼ cup celery, finely chopped

In medium saucepan mix gelatin, sugar, and salt; add ½ cup cold water. Stir over low heat till gelatin and sugar are dissolved. Stir in ¾ cup water, orange juice, lemon juice, vinegar, and food coloring; chill till partially set.

Fold in remaining ingredients; turn into 3½-cup mold. Chill till firm. Serves 6.

BLENDER CUCUMBER SALAD

88 calories / serving

Pass yogurt dressing with cucumber mold—

Peel 1 large cucumber; halve lengthwise and remove seeds. Slice cucumber into blender container; cover. Blend on high speed till puréed. Stop blender, as needed, to push cucumber down from side of container. Add water to purée, if necessary, to make 1 cup.

In medium saucepan combine 1 envelope unflavored gelatin (1 tablespoon) and 2 tablespoons sugar; add 1 cup unsweetened pineapple juice. Stir mixture over low heat till gelatin and sugar are dissolved. Add puréed cucumber, 4 teaspoons lemon juice, and 1 to 2 drops yellow food coloring. Chill till partially thickened; stirring occasionally. Pour the cucumber mixture into a 3½-cup mold. Chill till firm.

Serve with *Yogurt Dressing:* Combine ¼ cup yogurt, 1 tablespoon low-calorie mayonnaise-type dressing, 1½ teaspoons sugar, and ½ teaspoon lemon juice. Chill. Serves 4.

The refreshing goodness of oranges, shredded cabbage, and chopped celery are molded into this glistening Orange Perfection Salad.

Serve to summer luncheon guests this glimmering Raspberry-Cheese Mold with its cottage cheese and salad dressing filling.

PINEAPPLE MOLD
55 calories / serving

Refreshing salad made with carbonated beverage—

- 1 20-ounce can crushed pineapple (juice pack)
  Low-calorie lemon-lime carbonated beverage
- 1 envelope unflavored gelatin (1 tablespoon)
- 1 tablespoon lemon juice
  Few drops green food coloring
- 1 8½-ounce can unsweetened grapefruit sections, drained and cut up
- ¼ cup shredded cucumber, well drained

Drain pineapple, reserving juice. Add carbonated beverage (about 1⅓ cups) to reserved juice to make 2 cups. Soften gelatin in ½ *cup* of the mixture; stir over low heat till gelatin is dissolved. Stir in remaining juice mixture, lemon juice, and food coloring; chill till partially set. Fold in remaining ingredients; pour into 4½-cup mold. Chill till firm. Serves 8.

RASPBERRY-CHEESE MOLD
101 calories / serving

Colorful red and white ring mold is fun to make—

Add 1 cup water to one 10-ounce package frozen raspberries; heat to boiling. Remove from heat. Add one ⅞-ounce package low-calorie raspberry-flavored gelatin (2 envelopes); stir to dissolve. Sieve; add water to purée to make 4 cups. Pour *half* of the mixture into 6½-cup ring mold (leave remainder at room temperature); chill until the mixture is *almost* firm.

Soften 1 teaspoon unflavored gelatin in ½ cup cold water; heat and stir to dissolve. Mix 1½ cups small curd cream-style cottage cheese and ¼ cup low-calorie mayonnaise-type dressing. Add softened gelatin and ½ cup diced celery; mix well. Pour over berry layer. Chill till *almost* firm. Pour reserved berry mixture over cheese layer. Chill till firm. Serves 8.

SUNSHINE APPLE MOLD
80 calories / serving

Releases a mouth-watering cider aroma—

Thoroughly drain one 8¾-ounce can crushed pineapple; reserve syrup. Add apple juice (about 1⅔ cups) to reserved syrup to equal 2 cups. In saucepan soften 1 envelope unflavored gelatin (1 tablespoon) in juice mixture; stir over low heat till gelatin is dissolved. Stir in a few drops yellow food coloring; chill till partially set. Fold in the well-drained, crushed pineapple together with 1 cup chopped, unpeeled apple. Then turn the mixture into a 3½-cup mold. Chill till firm. To serve, unmold the salad on a lettuce-lined plate. Makes 6 servings.

SAUERKRAUT SALAD
39 calories / serving

Poppy seeds top crispy salad—

Combine one 16-ounce can sauerkraut, drained and snipped; 1 cup shredded carrot; ¼ cup chopped green pepper; and 2 tablespoons sliced green onion. Mix ¼ cup low-calorie Italian salad dressing and ½ teaspoon poppy seeds; add to vegetables and toss. Chill thoroughly. Serve in lettuce cups. Makes 6 servings.

*Keep calories
low in salad
dressings*

Retain low calorie count of salads—toss crisp, green salads with lemon juice, vinegar, or cream-style cottage cheese before serving.

CARROT-ORANGE SALAD

59 calories / serving

As pictured opposite contents page—

Cut 1 pound carrots into ½-inch slices. Cook in boiling water till crisp-tender, about 8 to 10 minutes; drain. Slice 3 thin slices from end of 1 unpeeled orange. Halve slices; add to carrots.

Squeeze remaining orange to make ¼ cup juice. Combine ½ cup low-calorie Italian salad dressing, orange juice, 2 tablespoons sliced green onion with tops, 1 tablespoon snipped parsley, ½ teaspoon grated orange peel, and ¼ teaspoon salt; stir into carrots. Cover and chill. Serve in lettuce cups with dressing. Serves 6.

DILLY TOMATO SLICES

33 calories / serving

Topped with dill-marinated cucumbers—

- ⅓ cup low-calorie Italian salad dressing
- ¼ cup water
- ½ teaspoon dried dillweed
- ½ teaspoon salt
- ⅛ teaspoon pepper

. . .

- 1 large cucumber, unpeeled
- 3 medium tomatoes, sliced
  Bibb lettuce leaves

Combine salad dressing, water, dillweed, salt, and pepper. Using a vegetable parer, slice cucumber *paper-thin* into shallow dish. Add marinade; cover and chill 6 hours or overnight.

To serve, arrange tomato slices atop Bibb lettuce leaves on serving platter or individual plates. Spoon on marinated cucumbers and marinade. Makes 6 servings.

ARTICHOKE-FRUIT SALAD

62 calories / serving

Pink grapefruit adds delicate color—

- 1 14-ounce can artichoke hearts, drained
- ¼ cup low-calorie Italian salad dressing
- 2 tablespoons vinegar
- 1 teaspoon Worcestershire sauce
- 1 tablespoon snipped parsley
- 3 cups torn iceberg lettuce
- 2 cups torn romaine
- 1 cup torn curly endive
- 2 pink grapefruit, peeled and sectioned

Halve artichokes. Combine salad dressing, next 3 ingredients, ½ teaspoon salt, and dash pepper; mix well. Pour over artichokes; chill, covered, 3 to 4 hours or overnight. In large bowl combine remaining ingredients. Add artichokes with dressing; toss. Makes 8 servings.

Have fun making Artichoke-Fruit Salad—toss assorted crisp greens and grapefruit sections with marinated artichoke hearts.

BROCCOLI SALAD BOWL

95 calories / serving

Marinate cooked broccoli spears in a peppy dill pickle dressing mixture—

Trim ends of 1 pound broccoli; peel stems if tough. Cook in 1 inch salted water till crisp-tender, about 10 to 12 minutes; drain thoroughly. Combine ¾ cup low-calorie French-style salad dressing; ¼ cup finely chopped dill pickle; ¼ cup minced green pepper; 2 tablespoons snipped parsley; and 1 tablespoon drained capers. Stir in 2 hard-cooked eggs, diced. Spoon dressing mixture over broccoli spears; cover and chill several hours or overnight. Serve broccoli on lettuce leaves. Makes 6 servings.

ASPARAGUS VINAIGRETTE

74 calories / serving

Complemented by a wine-flavored dressing—

    1 10-ounce package frozen asparagus
        spears
            . . .
    ½ cup low-calorie Italian salad
        dressing
    2 tablespoons dry sauterne
    2 tablespoons finely sliced green
        onion
    2 tablespoons finely chopped green
        pepper
    1 tablespoon finely snipped parsley
    1 tablespoon drained pickle relish
            . . .
    2 small tomatoes, chilled
        Lettuce leaves

Cook asparagus according to package directions; drain. Combine Italian salad dressing, sauterne, sliced green onion, chopped green pepper, parsley, and pickle relish; mix well.

Arrange asparagus spears in shallow dish; pour salad dressing mixture over all. Cover and chill several hours or overnight; occasionally spoon dressing mixture over spears.

To serve, drain asparagus spears, reserving salad dressing mixture. Slice tomatoes. For each salad, arrange a few asparagus spears atop a lettuce leaf; top with a few tomato slices. Spoon a little of the reserved salad dressing mixture over each salad. Makes 4 servings.

HERBED BEAN SALAD

50 calories / serving

Crushed oregano leaves add piquant flavor—

    1 9-ounce package frozen cut green
        beans *or* one 9-ounce package
        frozen Italian green beans
    1 cup thinly sliced celery
    1 onion, sliced and separated into
        rings
            . . .
    ⅓ cup low-calorie French-style salad
        dressing
    1 tablespoon finely chopped canned
        pimiento
    ¼ to ½ teaspoon dried oregano
        leaves, crushed
        Dash salt
            . . .
    Lettuce cups

Cook green beans according to package directions; drain. In shallow dish combine green beans, thinly sliced celery, and onions rings.

Blend together French-style salad dressing, chopped pimiento, oregano, and salt; toss with vegetable mixture. Cover; chill several hours or overnight, stirring occasionally.

To serve, spoon vegetable mixture and dressing into lettuce cups. Makes 5 servings.

BEAN AND CARROT SALAD

83 calories / serving

Arrange or toss the vegetables for serving—

    1 8-ounce can cut green beans
    1 8-ounce can sliced carrots
    1 8-ounce can red kidney beans
    1 small onion, thinly sliced
    2 tablespoons chopped celery
    2 tablespoons chopped green pepper
    1 tablespoons snipped parsley
    ¾ cup low-calorie Italian salad
        dressing

Drain canned vegetables. Arrange canned vegetables, onion, and celery in shallow dish. Sprinkle with green pepper and parsley. Pour low-calorie Italian salad dressing over vegetable mixture. Cover. Refrigerate several hours or overnight. Makes 6 servings.

TOMATO-CURRY DRESSING
25 calories / tablespoon

A brightly colored dressing with a superb flavor—

- 1 tablespoon cornstarch
- 1 tablespoon sugar
- 3/4 teaspoon curry powder
- 1/2 teaspoon paprika
- 1/4 teaspoon salt
- 3/4 cup pineapple juice
- 1/4 cup water
- 1/4 cup catsup
- 2 tablespoons salad oil
- 1 tablespoon vinegar

In small saucepan combine cornstarch, sugar, curry powder, paprika, and salt. Gradually blend pineapple juice and water into cornstarch mixture. Cook and stir till thick and bubbly; cook and stir 1 minute longer. Remove from heat; stir in catsup, oil, and vinegar. Chill. Serve over main dish salads. Makes 1 1/4 cups.

BLUE CHEESE DRESSING
18 calories / tablespoon

A creamy dressing made in the blender—

- 1 cup cream-style cottage cheese
- 1/3 cup water
- 2 tablespoons blue cheese, crumbled
- 1 teaspoon Worcestershire sauce

Put cottage cheese, water, blue cheese, and Worcestershire into blender container; cover. Blend till smooth. Chill. Makes about 1 cup.

BERRY-YOGURT DRESSING
9 calories / tablespoon

Fresh strawberries make a colorful dressing—

- 1 cup yogurt
- 1 cup fresh strawberries
- 1 tablespoon sugar
- 1/4 teaspoon ground cinnamon

Put yogurt, strawberries, sugar, and cinnamon in blender container. Cover and blend till strawberries are puréed and sugar is dissolved. Chill. Serve over fruit salads. Makes 1 1/2 cups.

CHILI-CHEESE DRESSING
25 calories / tablespoon

A dieter's version of Thousand Island dressing—

- 1 3-ounce package Neufchâtel cheese, softened
- 1/4 cup chili sauce
- 1 teaspoon prepared horseradish
- 2 tablespoons finely chopped green pepper

In bowl blend together cheese, chili sauce, and horseradish. Stir in green pepper; chill. Serve over seafood salads. Makes 2/3 cup.

COTTAGE-DILL DRESSING
16 calories / tablespoon

Dill pickle adds crunch as well as flavor—

- 1 cup cream-style cottage cheese
- 1 tablespoon lemon juice
- 3 tablespoons finely chopped dill pickle
- 1 tablespoon finely chopped onion

Put cottage cheese, lemon juice, and 1/3 cup water into blender; cover. Blend smooth. Stir in pickle and onion. Chill. Makes 1 cup.

COOKED SALAD DRESSING
22 calories / tablespoon

An excellent way to dress coleslaw—

- 2 tablespoons all-purpose flour
- 2 tablespoons sugar
- 1 teaspoon salt
- 1 teaspoon dry mustard
- 3/4 cup skim milk
- 2 slightly beaten egg yolks
- 2 tablespoons lemon juice
- 2 tablespoons vinegar

In small saucepan combine flour, sugar, salt, and dry mustard; gradually blend in milk. Cook and stir over medium heat till thick and bubbly. Stir a moderate amount of hot mixture into yolks; return to saucepan. Cook and stir over low heat for 1 minute. Stir in lemon juice and vinegar; chill. Makes about 1 cup.

SLENDERIZING SANDWICHES

FRUIT WHEELS
140 calories / serving

Bagels are spread with softened cream cheese—

Split and toast 2 bagels. Spread with 1 tablespoon cream cheese, softened; sprinkle with ground cinnamon. Thinly slice 1 fresh medium peach and ½ medium banana; dip peach and banana slices in ascorbic acid color keeper or lemon juice to prevent darkening. To assemble, arrange sliced fruit with 4 thin slices honeydew melon atop bagels. Makes 4 servings.

CUCUMBER SANDWICHES
106 calories / serving

For easy eating, serve with knife and fork—

Combine ¼ cup vinegar, 2 tablespoons water, 1 teaspoon sugar, ¼ teaspoon salt, ¼ teaspoon dried dillweed, and dash pepper; add 1 large unpeeled cucumber, thinly sliced. Cover and chill 3 hours; stir occasionally. Drain.
    Spread 4 slices firm-textured white bread with 4 teaspoons butter. Top with cucumber and 4 radishes, thinly sliced. Serves 4.

CHICKEN OPEN-FACES
139 calories / serving

Make-ahead chilled dressing adds smooth touch—

Mix 2 tablespoons all-purpose flour, 1 tablespoon sugar, 1 teaspoon dry mustard, ½ teaspoon salt, and dash cayenne; stir in 2 slightly beaten egg yolks and ¾ cup skim milk. Cook and stir over very low heat till thick and bubbly. Stir in 3 tablespoons vinegar; chill.
    Drain and slice one 5-ounce can water chestnuts. Roll edges of a few water chestnuts in paprika; set aside. Spread 8 slices whole wheat bread with some of the dressing; top *each* slice with 5 sprigs watercress, 1 slice cooked chicken, and a few remaining water chestnuts. Top with a few slices paprika-edged water chestnuts. Pass remaining dressing. Makes 8 servings.

HAM AND SALAD ROLLS
207 calories / serving

Ham slices encircle a crisp salad—

> 4 frankfurter buns, split
> 4 teaspoons prepared mustard
> 1 cup shredded lettuce
> ¼ cup chopped cucumber
> 2 tablespoons low-calorie French-style salad dressing
> 8 thin slices boiled ham
> 4 dill pickle strips

Spread cut sides of buns with mustard. Mix lettuce, cucumber, and dressing. Place ¼ of the mixture at one end of a stack of 2 ham slices; top with *1* pickle. Roll up jelly-roll fashion; secure with wooden picks. Place in bun. Repeat for remaining sandwiches. Serves 4.

COTTAGE CHEESE-WICHES
145 calories / serving

Crunchy, summer sandwich with caraway seed—

> 1½ cups small curd cream-style cottage cheese
> ½ cup diced celery
> ¼ cup shredded carrot
> ¼ cup chopped radish
> ½ teaspoon caraway seed
> 6 slices thinly sliced white bread
> 1 tablespoon butter, softened
> 6 lettuce leaves

Mash cheese with fork; stir in celery, carrot, radish, and caraway. Chill. Spread bread with butter; top with lettuce. Spread *each* sandwich with ⅓ cup of the cheese mixture. Serves 6.

Choose a tempting calorie-saver

Select from, top to bottom, Fruit Wheel, → Cucumber Sandwich, Chicken Open-Face, Ham and Salad Roll, or Cottage Cheese-Wich for a light and satisfying lunch.

SHRIMP STACK-UPS
156 calories / serving

A heaping sandwich with a low calorie count—

2 4½-ounce cans shrimp, drained, deveined, and chopped
1 tablespoon lemon juice
¼ cup diced celery
2 tablespoons chopped sweet pickle
2 tablespoons thinly sliced green onion
¼ teaspoon salt
Dash pepper
⅓ cup low-calorie mayonnaise-type dressing

• • •

3 English muffins, split and toasted
6 leaves Boston lettuce
6 tomato slices
1 hard-cooked egg, sliced

In small bowl sprinkle shrimp with lemon juice; add diced celery, chopped sweet pickle, sliced green onion, salt, pepper, and mayonnaise-type dressing. Mix gently; chill.

To assemble, top *each* muffin half with lettuce leaf and *1* tomato slice. Spoon about ⅓ cup of the shrimp mixture atop tomato slices. Garnish with egg slices. Makes 6 sandwiches.

DELUXE CRAB BROIL
139 calories / serving

Cheesy crab mixture served on English muffin—

1 7½-ounce can crab meat, drained, flaked, and cartilage removed
¼ cup low-calorie mayonnaise-type dressing
1 ounce shredded process American cheese (¼ cup)
¼ cup finely chopped celery
1 tablespoon chopped canned pimiento
2 teaspoons lemon juice
3 English muffins, split and toasted

In bowl combine crab, dressing, cheese, celery, pimiento, and lemon juice; mix well. Spread about ¼ *cup* of the crab mixture atop *each* muffin half. Broil 4 to 5 inches from heat till cheese melts, about 2 to 3 minutes. Garnish with parsley, if desired. Serves 6.

LOW-CALORIE
COOKING TIP

Sandwiches are an easy low-calorie lunch or snack

Serve sandwiches open-face to eliminate a second bread slice. Lightly spread bread with softened or whipped butter or margarine. (Softened or whipped butter spreads easily so less is needed than with firm spreads.) Top bread with remaining sandwich ingredients.

TUNA SALAD SANDWICH
157 calories / serving

A cool classic for a family lunch—

Mix one 6½-ounce can water-pack tuna, drained; ⅓ cup cream-style cottage cheese; ⅓ cup chopped celery; 1 tablespoon chopped sweet pickle; 1 tablespoon chopped onion; 1 tablespoon low-calorie mayonnaise-type dressing; and ¼ teaspoon salt. Spread 4 slices rye bread with 4 teaspoons low-calorie mayonnaise-type dressing. Top *each* slice with lettuce leaf and 1 slice tomato. Sprinkle with salt. Spoon tuna mixture atop tomatoes. Serves 4.

SALMON SANDWICH
146 calories / serving

Pink salmon has fewer calories than red salmon—

1 7¾-ounce can pink salmon, drained, flaked, and bones removed
⅓ cup low-calorie mayonnaise-type dressing
1 5-ounce can water chestnuts, drained and finely chopped
1 tablespoon sliced green onion
1 teaspoon soy sauce
1 teaspoon lemon juice
6 slices rye bread
6 cherry tomatoes

In bowl combine salmon, mayonnaise-type dressing, water chestnuts, onion, soy sauce, and lemon juice; mix thoroughly. Spread salmon mixture on bread slices. Garnish each sandwich with tomato; serve open-face. Serves 6.

DEVILED HAM BURGERS

251 calories / serving

Topped with radish and cucumber slices—

In bowl combine 1 beaten egg, ⅓ cup skim milk, ½ cup soft bread crumbs, and ¼ cup chopped green onion. Add 2 cups ground cooked ham; mix well. Shape into 6 patties. Brown patties on both sides in 1 tablespoon butter.

Place patties atop 3 English muffins, split and toasted. Top with 12 thin slices unpeeled cucumber and 2 or 3 radishes, thinly sliced.

Pass hot *Horseradish Sauce:* In saucepan melt 2 tablespoons butter. Stir in 2 tablespoons all-purpose flour and ¼ teaspoon salt. Add 1⅓ cups skim milk. Cook and stir till thick and bubbly. Remove from heat; stir in 1 teaspoon prepared horseradish. Serves 6.

OPEN-FACE BEEFBURGERS

232 calories / serving

A calorie counter's version of a cheeseburger—

Toast 4 slices sandwich-style rye bread on one side. Divide and spread ½ pound lean ground beef on untoasted side of bread, spreading to edges. Sprinkle with salt. Broil 3 inches from heat, 5 to 6 minutes. Top *each* sandwich with 1 thin slice onion and 2 thin slices tomato. Broil 2 minutes more; remove from broiler. Halve 2 slices mozzarella cheese (3 ounces); place cheese slices atop sandwiches. Return sandwiches to broiler till cheese melts. Makes 4 sandwiches.

HOT CHEESE-EGG SANDWICH

185 calories / serving

Excellent idea for a weekend brunch—

In medium bowl combine 4 hard-cooked eggs, chopped; ¼ cup low-calorie mayonnaise-type dressing; 2 tablespoons sweet pickle relish; 2 tablespoons chopped green onion; and 1 tablespoon prepared mustard. Spread on 6 slices white bread, toasted. Broil 4 inches from heat till heated through, about 3 to 4 minutes.

Halve 3 slices mozzarella cheese (4½ ounces). Top *each* sandwich with cheese slice and 1 thin slice tomato; sprinkle with salt. Return to broiler till cheese melts. Makes 6 sandwiches.

Pass a platter of colorful Deviled Ham Burgers around and watch them quickly disappear. Serve with zesty Horseradish Sauce.

HAM-ASPARAGUS BROIL

184 calories / serving

Melted cheese drizzles over ham and asparagus—

- 1 10-ounce package frozen asparagus spears
- 4 slices white bread, toasted
- 2 teaspoons prepared mustard
- 4 slices boiled ham
- 2 ounces process Swiss cheese, shredded (½ cup)
- 2 tablespoons chopped green onion
- 1 tablespoon chopped canned pimiento

Cook asparagus spears according to package directions; drain well. Keep warm. Spread mustard on one side of each slice toast. Place ham slices on bread; arrange hot asparagus spears atop ham. Toss together shredded cheese, chopped green onion, and chopped pimiento. Sprinkle cheese mixture over asparagus. Broil 5 inches from heat till cheese melts, about 2 to 3 minutes. Makes 4 sandwiches.

LIGHT AND SATISFYING DESSERTS

LEMON-BLUEBERRY FLUFF

76 calories / serving

Prepare sauce with fresh berries when available—

- 1 3-ounce package lemon-flavored gelatin
- 1 cup boiling water
- ¼ teaspoon grated lemon peel
- 2 tablespoons lemon juice
- ¾ cup cold water
- 2 egg whites

• • •

- 1 9-ounce carton frozen unsweetened blueberries, thawed (1½ cups)
- 1 tablespoon cornstarch
- ½ cup cold water
- 2 tablespoons sugar
  Few drops vanilla

In large bowl dissolve gelatin in boiling water. Stir in lemon peel, lemon juice, and ¾ cup cold water. Chill till partially set.

Add unbeaten egg whites to gelatin mixture. Beat with electric mixer till mixture is light and fluffy, about 1 to 2 minutes. Pour into eight 5-ounce custard cups. Chill till firm. (Slight separation into layers may occur.)

Meanwhile, in saucepan crush ½ *cup* of the blueberries. Blend together cornstarch and ½ cup cold water. Add cornstarch mixture and sugar to crushed blueberries. Cook over medium heat, stirring constantly, till mixture is thick and bubbly; cook and stir 1 minute longer. Remove sauce from heat; stir in remaining blueberries and vanilla. Chill sauce.

To serve, unmold lemon fluff in individual dessert dishes. Spoon a little blueberry sauce over each dessert. Makes 8 servings.

A glamorous finale

← Capped with a striking, fresh-flavored berry sauce, Lemon-Blueberry Fluff is sure to bring raves from both dieters and non-dieters.

HONEYDEW-BERRY PARFAITS

80 calories / serving

As pictured opposite section introduction—

- 2½ cups fresh strawberries
- 1 tablespoon sugar
- 1 ripe large banana, mashed
- ½ cup yogurt
- 2 teaspoons sugar
- ⅛ teaspoon ground cinnamon
- 2 cups fresh honeydew melon, diced

Reserve 6 berries; quarter remaining berries. Sprinkle quartered berries with 1 tablespoon sugar. Mix banana and next 3 ingredients; blend well. Arrange melon in bottom of 6 parfait glasses; spoon *half* of the yogurt mixture over melon. Top with sweetened berries; spoon remaining yogurt mixture over berries. Garnish with reserved whole berries. Serves 6.

STRAWBERRIES JULIET

78 calories / serving

A dieter's dream of strawberries with cream—

Using 2½ cups fresh strawberries, chilled, crush ¼ *cup* of the berries; halve remaining berries. Combine crushed berries; ⅓ cup frozen whipped dessert topping, thawed; ⅓ cup yogurt; and 1 tablespoon sugar. Spoon halved berries into 4 sherbet glasses; top with strawberry-yogurt mixture. Makes 4 servings.

AMBROSIA

110 calories / serving

As pictured on front cover—

Peel and section 4 medium oranges over bowl to catch juices. To oranges and juice add 2 ripe medium bananas, sliced, and 3 maraschino cherries, quartered. Toss. Sprinkle with 2 tablespoons shredded coconut. Makes 6 servings.

Use canned fruit packed in juice when available

To economize on calories, purchase juice-packed pineapple that has 20 calories less than an equal serving packed in syrup.

RASPBERRY-YOGURT FLUFF

74 calories / serving

Delicate almond flavor accents this dessert—

  1 10-ounce package frozen raspberries
  1 tablespoon cornstarch
  1 8-ounce carton yogurt
  ¼ teaspoon almond extract
     Few drops red food coloring
  1 egg white
  ¼ teaspoon cream of tartar

Thaw berries; drain, reserving syrup. Add water to syrup to make 1 cup. In saucepan blend syrup mixture with cornstarch. Cook and stir over medium heat till thick and bubbly. Remove from heat; cool. Stir in yogurt, extract, and food coloring. Fold in berries. Beat egg white with cream of tartar till stiff peaks form. Gently fold into yogurt mixture. Spoon into dessert dishes. Chill. Makes 6 servings.

GRAPEFRUIT-BERRY COMPOTE

89 calories / serving

Spicy duo can also be served as an appetizer—

  1 10-ounce package frozen raspberries
  2 tablespoons sugar
  3 inches stick cinnamon
  ½ teaspoon whole cloves
  2 large white grapefruit

Thaw berries; drain, reserving syrup. Mix syrup, ¼ cup water, sugar, cinnamon, and cloves; bring to boiling. Reduce heat. Simmer, uncovered, 10 minutes; strain. Peel and section grapefruit; place in 10x6x1¾-inch baking dish. Top with berries; pour syrup over fruits. Cover; chill several hours or overnight. Serves 6.

RHUBARB-STRAWBERRY BOWL

56 calories / serving

Fresh fruit served in a blushing red sauce—

In saucepan combine ¾ pound fresh rhubarb, cut in 1-inch slices (3 cups); ⅓ cup sugar; and 1 cup water. Bring to boiling; reduce heat. Simmer till almost tender, about 2 minutes.

Remove from heat. Drain; reserve syrup. Add water to syrup to make 1¼ cups. Mix 1 tablespoon cornstarch, dash salt, and ¼ cup cold water; add to syrup mixture. Cook and stir till thick and bubbly. Cook and stir 2 minutes more. Remove from heat; cool slightly. Stir in 1 teaspoon lemon juice and few drops red food coloring. Gently stir in rhubarb and 2 cups fresh strawberries, sliced. Chill. Serves 8.

YOGURT-FRUIT MEDLEY

86 calories / serving

Versatile dessert that doubles as a salad—

Drain one 15¼-ounce can pineapple chunks (juice pack), reserving juice. In saucepan blend 2 teaspoons sugar with 2 teaspoons cornstarch; stir in reserved juice. Cook and stir over medium heat till thick and bubbly. Reduce heat; cook and stir 1 minute more.

Remove from heat; stir in ½ teaspoon vanilla. Cool 10 minutes without stirring. Blend mixture into ½ cup yogurt. Add pineapple; 3 medium oranges, peeled, sectioned, and coarsely chopped; and 1 cup seedless green grapes, halved. Mix lightly. Chill. Makes 8 servings.

APPLE-GINGER BAKE

113 calories / serving

Gingersnaps spice up this apple dessert—

Peel, core, and slice 5 apples; place *half* of the apples in bottom of 8x8x2-inch pan. Mix 8 gingersnaps, crushed (½ cup), and 2 tablespoons brown sugar. Sprinkle *half* of the crumb mixture over apple slices. Top with remaining apples; sprinkle with remaining crumbs.

Mix ⅓ cup water and 1 tablespoon lemon juice; pour evenly over apple mixture. Bake, covered, at 375° till apples are tender, 40 to 45 minutes. Serve warm. Makes 6 servings.

BAKED CRIMSON PEARS
69 calories / serving

Delicious served either warm or chilled—

Peel, halve, and core 4 fresh medium pears; place in 1-quart casserole. Mix 1 cup low-calorie cranberry juice cocktail, 3 inches stick cinnamon, and 10 drops red food coloring; bring to boiling. Pour over pears. Bake, covered, at 350° for 10 minutes. Turn pears; bake, covered, 10 minutes. Turn pears; bake, uncovered, till tender, 5 to 10 minutes more. Remove cinnamon stick. Serve in juice. Serves 8.

BAKED ORANGE CUPS
107 calories / serving

Festive enough for a party luncheon dessert—

Remove tops of 4 medium oranges. With grapefruit knife, scoop out pulp and reserve. Dice reserved pulp; toss with ½ cup seedless green grapes, halved, and dash bitters.

Spoon fruit into orange shells. Place in 10x6x1¾-inch baking dish. Pour a little water around oranges. Bake at 325° for 25 minutes. Sprinkle with 2 tablespoons flaked coconut. Bake 8 to 10 minutes more. Makes 4 servings.

Impart a rosy red color to pears as they bake, with low-calorie cranberry juice cocktail and food coloring. This eye-catching dessert, Baked Crimson Pears, is certain to be a winner.

SPICY PEACH COMPOTE
63 calories / serving

Use canned peaches when fresh aren't available—

- 3 large fresh peaches
- 2 teaspoons cornstarch
- 2 tablespoons sugar
- ½ of 6-ounce can pineapple-orange juice concentrate, thawed (⅓ cup)
- ½ teaspoon grated orange peel
- 4 inches stick cinnamon
- 5 whole cloves

Peel, halve, and pit peaches; sprinkle with ascorbic acid color keeper or lemon juice mixed with water to prevent darkening. In saucepan mix cornstarch, sugar, and ¼ teaspoon salt. Stir in concentrate, ⅔ cup water, peel, cinnamon, and cloves. Cook and stir till thick and bubbly; cook and stir 2 minutes more. Pour hot mixture over peaches; chill. Remove spices before serving. Makes 6 servings.

MARINATED FRUIT
85 calories / serving

A delicious dessert for an outdoor barbecue—

- 1 20-ounce can pineapple chunks (juice pack)
- 1 medium apple
- 1 fresh medium pear
- 1 medium nectarine
- 2 tablespoons orange juice concentrate, thawed
- 1 tablespoon honey
- 1 teaspoon snipped fresh mint *or* 1 teaspoon dried mint flakes, crushed

Drain pineapple; reserve juice. Remove cores from unpeeled apple and pear; pit nectarine. Cut fruits into chunks. Mix fruits in shallow dish. Mix reserved juice with remaining ingredients; pour over fruits. Stir to mix. Cover; marinate in refrigerator 2 to 3 hours; stir occasionally. Serve with marinade. Serves 8.

Start or end a meal with refreshing Fresh Fruit Aloha, a colorful, cool medley of fresh fruits—pineapple, papaya, and strawberries—sprinkled lightly with lime juice and sugar.

SEASONING GUIDE FOR FRUITS

Spices and flavorings add variety to fresh fruit, baked fruit desserts, and compotes without increasing calories. Experiment with different spices and flavorings by adding a small amount to individual fruits or fruit mixtures. Or, use ground spices as a garnish and sprinkle lightly over fruit or baked desserts before serving.

Apples	allspice, anise, caraway seed, cardamom, cinnamon, cloves, dill, ginger, mint, nutmeg, almond extract, citrus extracts
Bananas	allspice, cinnamon, ginger, nutmeg
Berries	cinnamon, clove, ginger, nutmeg, rosemary, vanilla flavoring
Cherries	allspice, cloves, cinnamon, mace, mint, nutmeg, almond extract, brandy flavoring, rum flavoring, vanilla flavoring
Cranberries	allspice, cinnamon, cloves, ginger, nutmeg, rosemary, almond extract
Grapefruit	anise, cinnamon, ginger
Grapes	allspice, cinnamon, cloves
Melons	cardamom, ginger, mint
Oranges	allspice, anise, cinnamon, cloves, ginger, mace, nutmeg, rosemary
Peaches	allspice, cinnamon, cloves, ginger, nutmeg, rosemary, almond extract, brandy flavoring, maple flavoring, rum flavoring
Pears	allspice, anise, cinnamon, mint, nutmeg, maple flavoring
Pineapple	allspice, cardamom, cinnamon, cloves, coriander, mace, mint, nutmeg, rosemary, maple flavoring, vanilla flavoring
Plums	allspice, cinnamon, cloves, almond extract
Prunes	allspice, anise, cinnamon, cloves, ginger, nutmeg, almond extract, citrus extracts, maple flavoring
Rhubarb	cinnamon, ginger, nutmeg, rosemary, citrus extracts, vanilla flavoring
Strawberries	allspice, cinnamon, cloves, rosemary, vanilla flavoring

FRESH FRUIT ALOHA

81 calories / serving

Papaya lends a Polynesian flavor—

- 1 cup fresh pineapple chunks
- 1 papaya, peeled, seeded, and cubed
- ½ cup sliced fresh strawberries
- 1 teaspoon lime juice
- 2 tablespoons sugar

Combine pineapple, papaya, and strawberries; sprinkle with lime juice and *1 tablespoon* of the sugar. Chill thoroughly. To serve, sprinkle fruits with remaining sugar. Serves 4.

RASPBERRY-APPLE DESSERT

67 calories / serving

Sprinkle each serving with one teaspoon flaked coconut and increase calorie count by only seven—

Add 1½ cups boiling water to one 3-ounce package raspberry-flavored gelatin; stir to dissolve gelatin. Stir in 1 cup dietetic-pack applesauce; chill till mixture is partially set.

Beat 2 egg whites with dash salt till soft peaks form. Slowly add 2 tablespoons sugar; beat till stiff peaks form. Fold in gelatin mixture. Chill, if necessary, till mixture mounds. Spoon into sherbet glasses; chill. Serves 8.

PEACHY ORANGE ICE

74 calories / serving

Refreshing dessert for a warm summer day—

    1 12-ounce package frozen peach
        slices, partially thawed
    1 cup orange juice
    1 tablespoon lemon juice
    3 egg whites
      Dash salt
    3 tablespoons sugar

In blender container combine undrained peaches, orange juice, and lemon juice; blend till peaches are puréed, about 15 seconds.

Beat egg whites with dash salt till soft peaks form. Gradually add sugar, beating till stiff peaks form. Transfer peach purée to mixing bowl; gently fold beaten egg whites into peach purée. Freeze peach mixture in 4-cup refrigerator tray till mixture is *almost* firm.

Remove almost firm peach mixture to chilled bowl; beat well with rotary or electric beater. Return to refrigerator tray; freeze till mixture is firm. To serve, spoon frozen peach mixture into sherbet dishes. Makes 8 servings.

Cool and satisfying Blueberry Ice is a welcome low-calorie treat served at the end of a meal or as a refreshing afternoon snack.

LOW-CALORIE

COOKING TIP

Use a refrigerator tray to freeze low-calorie ices. When mixture is frozen, break into chunks with a fork. For whipped ices, transfer chunks to chilled bowl and beat till smooth. Return to tray and freeze till firm.

APRICOT-GRAPEFRUIT ICE

94 calories / serving

A streamlined dessert using only 3 ingredients—

Combine one 12-ounce can apricot nectar, 1 cup unsweetened grapefruit juice, and 2 tablespoons sugar; stir till sugar is dissolved. Freeze in 3-cup refrigerator tray till *almost* firm. With fork, break mixture into small pieces. Spoon into sherbets. Garnish with mint sprigs. Serve immediately. Makes 4 servings.

BLUEBERRY ICE

44 calories / serving

Delicate berry flavor in a chilly dessert—

    ¼ cup sugar
    ½ envelope unflavored gelatin
        (1½ teaspoons)
  1½ cups water
    1 9-ounce carton unsweetened frozen
        blueberries, thawed (1½ cups)
    3 tablespoons lemon juice

In saucepan combine sugar and gelatin; stir in *1 cup* of the water. Heat and stir over medium heat till sugar and gelatin dissolve.

Remove from heat; add remaining water, berries, and lemon juice. Freeze in 3-cup refrigerator tray till firm. Break into chunks; beat with electric mixer till smooth. Return to tray; freeze firm. Let stand at room temperature 5 to 10 minutes before serving. Serves 8.

CRANBERRY SHERBET

88 calories / serving

An excellent ending for a Thanksgiving Dinner—

In saucepan combine ½ cup sugar; ½ envelope unflavored gelatin (1½ teaspoons); and dash salt. Stir in 1 cup low-calorie cranberry juice cocktail. Heat and stir over medium heat till sugar and gelatin dissolve. Remove from heat.

Stir in additional 1 cup low-calorie cranberry juice cocktail and 1 tablespoon lemon juice. Freeze in 3-cup refrigerator tray till firm. Break into chunks; in chilled bowl beat with electric mixer till smooth. Return cranberry mixture to tray; freeze firm. Makes 6 servings.

RASPBERRY ICE

90 calories / serving

Delicious served on a fresh fruit plate—

Thaw two 10-ounce packages frozen raspberries; sieve. Set aside. Dissolve one 3-ounce package raspberry-flavored gelatin in 1 cup boiling water; stir in ¾ cup cold water, ¼ cup orange juice, and 1 tablespoon lemon juice. Stir in sieved raspberries. Freeze raspberry mixture in two 4-cup refrigerator trays till mixture is firm.

Break into chunks; in chilled bowl beat *half* of the mixture with an electric beater till smooth. Return to tray; repeat with remaining mixture. Freeze firm. Makes 10 servings.

GLORIFIED RICE

98 calories / serving

A fruit-filled version of a homey favorite—

In saucepan combine ½ cup water, ⅓ cup uncooked packaged precooked rice, and ¼ teaspoon salt; stir to moisten. Bring to boiling; cover. Simmer 5 minutes. Remove from heat; let stand 5 minutes. Stir in one 20-ounce can crushed pineapple (juice pack), drained. Cool.

Meanwhile, sprinkle 1 medium banana, sliced, with 2 teaspoons lemon juice. Stir banana slices into cooled rice mixture. Combine ½ cup yogurt, 1 tablespoon sugar, and 1 teaspoon vanilla; fold into rice mixture. Chill.

Spoon rice mixture into serving dishes. Top with 1 cup halved strawberries. Serves 8.

Rice Pudding Royale, a delightful version of a popular dessert, is made with cottage cheese. Top with shredded orange peel.

RICE PUDDING ROYALE

112 calories / serving

Cottage cheese provides a creamy texture—

   1 cup skim milk
   ½ cup uncooked long-grain rice
   ⅛ cup sugar
   ½ teaspoon grated lemon peel
   ¼ teaspoon grated orange peel
   1 teaspoon vanilla
   ¼ teaspoon almond extract
   ¾ cup cream-style cottage cheese

In top of double boiler combine milk and 2 cups water; add rice, sugar, and ¼ teaspoon salt. Cook, covered, over boiling water for 1 hour; stir often. Uncover; cook till thickened, 30 to 40 minutes. Remove from heat; stir in grated peels and flavorings. Chill thoroughly.

Beat cottage cheese; stir into rice mixture. Spoon into dessert dishes; sprinkle with shredded orange peel, if desired. Makes 8 servings.

LOW-CALORIE
COOKING TIP

Use skim milk in cooking and as a beverage

Substitute skim milk for whole milk to reduce calories. One cup whole milk contains 160 calories, 1 cup fortified skim milk provides 105 calories, and 1 cup milk prepared from nonfat dry milk powder has only 82 calories.

RASPBERRY BAVARIAN MOLD

60 calories / serving

Scrumptious, yet unbelievably low in calories—

Thaw one 10-ounce package frozen red raspberries; reserve 2 tablespoons berries for garnish. Drain remaining berries, reserving ½ cup syrup. Dissolve one ⅞-ounce package low-calorie raspberry-flavored gelatin (2 envelopes) in 1¼ cups boiling water. Stir in reserved ½ cup syrup, 1 tablespoon lemon juice, and dash salt. Chill till mixture is partially set.

Add ⅔ cup evaporated skim milk, chilled *icy cold*; beat at high speed with electric mixer till soft peaks form, about 4 minutes.

Fold in drained berries. Pour into 6½-cup mold. Chill till firm, 2 to 3 hours. Unmold; drizzle with reserved berries. Serves 8.

LIME SNOW

80 calories / serving

Light and colorful for a springtime luncheon—

In saucepan combine 1 envelope unflavored gelatin (1 tablespoon); ⅓ cup sugar; and ¼ teaspoon salt. Stir in 1¼ cups cold water. Stir over low heat till gelatin is dissolved.

Remove from heat. Add one 6-ounce can frozen limeade concentrate and ½ teaspoon grated lemon peel; stir to thaw. Chill till partially set. Turn into large bowl; add 2 unbeaten egg whites and 2 to 3 drops green food coloring. Beat at high speed with electric mixer till light and fluffy, about 1 to 2 minutes.

Pour into 5½-cup mold or eight 5-ounce custard cups. Chill till firm. (Slight separation into layers may occur.) Makes 8 servings.

MERINGUE-TOPPED PEACHES

97 calories / serving

Drizzle custard sauce over snow-capped peach halves for an elegant dessert—

- 1 16-ounce can dietetic-pack peach halves, drained (6 halves)
- 2 tablespoons frozen orange juice concentrate, thawed
- ½ teaspoon grated lemon peel
- 2 egg whites
- ¼ teaspoon vanilla
- 1 tablespoon sugar
   Custard Sauce

Place peaches, cut side up, in shallow baking dish. Mix concentrate and peel; spoon into peach halves. Beat egg whites with ¼ teaspoon salt and vanilla till soft peaks form. Gradually add sugar; beat till stiff peaks form.

Swirl meringue over peach halves. Bake at 400° till lightly browned, 6 to 8 minutes.

Prepare *Custard Sauce:* In saucepan mix 1 cup skim milk, 2 slightly beaten egg yolks, 2 tablespoons sugar, and dash salt. Cook and stir over medium heat till thick and mixture coats metal spoon. Stir in ½ teaspoon vanilla; chill. Spoon sauce over peaches. Makes 6 servings.

MOCHA CHIFFON

104 calories / serving

Rich, flavorful blend of cocoa and coffee—

In saucepan mix ½ cup sugar; 2 envelopes unflavored gelatin (2 tablespoons); 2 tablespoons unsweetened cocoa powder; 1 tablespoon instant coffee powder; and ½ teaspoon salt.

Combine 2½ cups skim milk, ½ cup water, and 3 beaten egg yolks. Stir milk mixture into gelatin mixture. Cook over medium heat, stirring constantly, till gelatin and sugar dissolve and mixture thickens slightly. Remove from heat. Chill mixture till partially set.

Beat together 3 egg whites, 1 teaspoon vanilla, and ¼ teaspoon cream of tartar till soft peaks form. Carefully fold gelatin mixture into egg whites. Chill till mixture mounds. Spoon into 6½-cup mold. Chill till firm.

To serve, unmold dessert onto serving plate. Sprinkle with 3 chocolate wafers, crushed (about ¼ cup). Makes 10 servings.

SNOW PUDDING
132 calories / serving

Velvety custard sauce is also good with fruit—

In saucepan combine ⅓ cup sugar, ⅛ teaspoon salt, and 2 teaspoons unflavored gelatin. Add ⅓ cup cold water. Stir over low heat to dissolve. Remove from heat; add ¼ cup cold water, ¼ teaspoon grated lemon peel, and 2 tablespoons lemon juice. Chill till partially set.

Turn into bowl; add 2 unbeaten egg whites. Beat with electric or rotary beater till mixture begins to hold its shape. Pour into five 5-ounce custard cups. Chill till firm. To serve, unmold. Drizzle with Custard Sauce. Top with low-calorie red jelly. Serves 5.

Custard Sauce: In heavy saucepan combine ¾ cup skim milk, 2 beaten egg yolks, 4 teaspoons sugar, and dash salt. Cook and stir over very low heat till mixture coats metal spoon. Remove from heat; cool immediately by placing pan in cold water. Stir several minutes; stir in ½ teaspoon vanilla. Chill.

PINEAPPLE-MINT DESSERT
79 calories / serving

Vary the color for each occasion—

Thoroughly drain one 20-ounce can crushed pineapple (juice pack), reserving 1 cup juice. In saucepan mix ¼ cup sugar and 1 envelope unflavored gelatin (1 tablespoon); stir in reserved juice. Stir over low heat till gelatin and sugar dissolve. Remove from heat; stir in ¼ teaspoon vanilla, several drops peppermint extract, few drops red *or* green food coloring, and pineapple. Chill mixture till partially set.

In mixing bowl combine ⅓ cup nonfat dry milk powder and ⅓ cup ice water; beat at high speed till stiff peaks form. Carefully fold in gelatin mixture. Chill, if necessary, till mixture mounds. Spoon into sherbet dishes. Chill till firm. Makes 8 servings.

Regal pudding dessert

Tart, red jelly adds the crowning touch to Snow Pudding. Mound puddings in colorful glass bowl or serve individually.

STREAMLINED BEVERAGES

APRICOT-PINEAPPLE FROST

61 calories / serving

Peppermint flavoring is the surprise—

In blender container combine one 12-ounce can apricot nectar, chilled; one 6-ounce can pineapple juice, chilled; and 1/2 teaspoon peppermint extract. Cover, blend a few seconds, till frothy. Pour over ice in glasses; garnish with mint sprigs, if desired. Makes 5 servings.

STRAWBERRY SHAKE

72 calories / serving

Looks and tastes like an ice cream shake—

    2 cups fresh *or* frozen unsweetened
        whole strawberries
  1 1/2 cups skim milk
    2 tablespoons sugar
      Dash ground cinnamon

If using fresh strawberries, halve larger berries; freeze in plastic bag. In blender container combine milk, sugar, and cinnamon; gradually add frozen berries. Blend on medium speed till smooth. Serve immediately. Serves 5.

CITRUS COOLER

50 calories / serving

Citrus foursome makes a sparkling drink—

    1 6-ounce can frozen grapefruit-
        orange concentrate, thawed
    2 cups cold water
      Dash bitters
  1 1/2 cups low-calorie lemon-lime
        carbonated beverage

In pitcher combine thawed grapefruit-orange concentrate, cold water, and dash bitters; chill thoroughly. Just before serving, carefully pour carbonated beverage down side of pitcher; stir gently with an up-and-down motion. Serve beverage over ice. Makes 6 servings.

APPLE-COT COOLER

61 calories / serving

Bitters add sophisticated flavor—

    2 cups apple juice
    1 12-ounce can apricot nectar
  1/4 cup lemon juice
  1/4 teaspoon bitters
    3 7-ounce bottles carbonated
        water, chilled
    8 thin lemon slices

In pitcher combine apple juice, apricot nectar, lemon juice, and bitters; chill. Just before serving, carefully pour carbonated water down side of pitcher. Stir gently with an up-and-down motion. Serve in ice-filled glasses. Garnish with lemon slices. Makes 8 servings.

RASPBERRY FIZZ

48 calories / serving

Fizz is a low-calorie lemon-lime beverage—

    1 12-ounce can pineapple juice,
        chilled
    1 10-ounce package frozen raspberries,
        thawed
    2 16-ounce bottles low-calorie lemon-
        lime carbonated beverage, chilled
      Mint sprigs

In blender container combine pineapple juice, berries, and 1/2 cup water. Blend on medium speed till berries are puréed; strain. Pour mixture into pitcher. Gradually pour carbonated beverage down side of pitcher, stirring with an up-and-down motion. Serve over ice. Garnish with mint sprigs. Makes 10 servings.

Cool and refreshing fruit duo

Blend Apricot-Pineapple Frost till a big →
frothy head appears. Pour into tall ice-filled tumblers and garnish with mint sprigs.

Watch your friends help themselves to a glassful of this Ruby Lemonade Punch at your next get-together. Serve it icy cold.

RUBY LEMONADE PUNCH

74 calories / serving

Float thin lemon slices atop brilliant red drink—

Stir one 6-ounce can frozen lemonade concentrate, thawed, into 1 quart low-calorie cranberry juice cocktail. Slowly add one 16-ounce bottle low-calorie lemon-lime carbonated beverage; stir gently with an up-and-down motion. Serve over ice. Garnish with lemon slices. Serves 8.

GRAPE-GRAPEFRUIT PUNCH

49 calories / serving

Regal purple drink with a grapefruit bite—

Combine 2 cups unsweetened grapefruit juice and one 6-ounce can frozen grape juice concentrate, thawed; chill. Just before serving, slowly add one 28-ounce bottle carbonated water, stirring with an up-and-down motion. Garnish with lemon slices, if desired. Makes 10 servings.

ORANGE-PINEAPPLE FROST

48 calories / serving

Electric blender does all the work—

    1 6-ounce can frozen pineapple-orange
        juice concentrate, thawed
    6 cups finely crushed ice

Place thawed concentrate in chilled blender. Add ice, 1 cup at a time, blending well after each addition. Stop blender several times and push ice down with rubber spatula. Serve in tall glasses with straws and spoons. Serves 6.

LIMEADE SLUSH

41 calories / serving

Colorful and refreshing icy drink for any day—

    2 16-ounce bottles low-calorie
        lemon-lime carbonated beverage
    1 6-ounce can frozen limeade
        concentrate, thawed
    Mint sprigs

Pour carbonated beverage into freezer trays or shallow pan; freeze firm. Break into chunks and crush. Pour thawed limeade concentrate into blender container; add frozen crushed beverage 1 cup at a time, blending well after each addition. Stop blender several times and push ice down with rubber spatula. Spoon into glasses. Garnish with mint sprigs. Makes 8 servings.

FRUITY LIME TEA

59 calories / serving

Frozen limeade gives fresh perky flavor—

    4 teaspoons instant tea powder
    ½ 6-ounce can frozen limeade
        concentrate, thawed (⅛ cup)
    1 12-ounce can pineapple juice
        (1½ cups)
    Few drops green food coloring

In pitcher dissolve instant tea powder in 2¼ cups cold water. Stir in limeade concentrate, pineapple juice, and green food coloring; chill. Serve over ice-filled glasses. Garnish with mint sprigs, if desired. Makes 6 servings.

LOW-CALORIE

COOKING TIP

Reduce calories in punches and fruit drinks by using low-calorie carbonated beverages. Just before serving, carefully pour carbonated beverage down the inside of the pitcher. Stir gently with an up-and-down motion.

SPICED ICED COFFEE

63 calories / serving

Add cola before serving for the fizz—

In blender container combine 1½ cups skim milk, 2 tablespoons sugar, 2 tablespoons instant coffee powder, and ¼ teaspoon ground cinnamon; blend till well mixed.

Just before serving, carefully add one 16-ounce bottle low-calorie cola beverage, chilled. Stir gently with an up-and-down motion. Serve over ice. Makes 6 servings.

MULLED CRANBERRY DRINK

66 calories / serving

An intriguing hot drink flavored with the right amount of spices—

   1 quart low-calorie cranberry
       juice cocktail (4 cups)
   1 18-ounce can pineapple juice
       (2¼ cups)
   1 teaspoon whole allspice
   1 teaspoon whole cloves
       Dash salt
       Dash ground nutmeg
   3 inches stick cinnamon

In large saucepan combine all ingredients; slowly bring mixture to boiling. Reduce heat; cover and simmer for 20 minutes. Remove from heat; pour juice mixture through strainer to remove whole spices. Makes 8 servings.

HOT SPICED TEA

77 calories / serving

A steaming hot tea with a fruity flavor—

In saucepan mix one 18-ounce can pineapple juice, 2 cups orange juice, 2 cups water, 4 teaspoons instant tea powder, 1 teaspoon whole allspice, and 3 inches stick cinnamon. Bring to boiling; reduce heat. Simmer, covered, for 15 minutes. Strain. Makes 8 servings.

MAPLE SKIMMER

77 calories / serving

Evaporated skim milk adds a nutritive note—

Dissolve 2 teaspoons instant coffee powder in 1¾ cups water. Add one 14½-ounce can evaporated skim milk, 2 tablespoons sugar, and ¾ teaspoon maple flavoring; stir. Serve over Coffee Ice Cubes. Makes 5 servings.

Coffee Ice Cubes: Stir together 1 teaspoon instant coffee powder for each 1 cup water. Freeze in ice cube trays.

Float frozen coffee ice cubes atop full-bodied Maple Skimmer. As they begin to melt, the flavored ice cubes add drinking enjoyment.

Calorie-Planned Menus

Need help in planning a sensible
weight control program?
Then learn the simplified method for
determining calorie needs.
Once you've got this under way,
use the Basic Four Menu Guide to
plan your daily menus.
Or, follow our weekly menu plan that
is tailored to your calorie
needs and designed with flavor,
appetite appeal, and
nutrition in mind. You'll discover
it's the fun way to
calorie-count and enjoy it.

**Inviting entrées, such as
Pepper Steak, served with fluffy rice,
lettuce wedge, and fruit make
appealing and satisfying diet fare.**

HOW TO PLAN LOW-CALORIE MENUS

A well-balanced diet is important regardless of whether the ultimate goal is to lose a few pounds or to maintain your present weight. Too often the chief concern of the overweight individual is that of reducing calories without regard for adequate nutrition. However, calories should not be lowered indiscriminately. The diet must still provide the essential nutrients for the body.

An overweight condition is most often the result of taking in more calories than the body needs. Likewise, a weight loss generally results when the caloric intake is lower than the caloric need. To balance these two factors, you must first know the number of calories required by the body. These needs are based upon your age, desirable weight, and the amount of your daily physical activity. Use the simplified method for figuring your daily caloric needs (see box below). Once this is known, you can work out a diet.

For example, approximately 3500 calories are needed to make 1 pound of fat body tissue. If the caloric intake is reduced by 500 calories per day (3500 per week), approximately 1 pound per week is lost. By lowering the daily caloric intake 1000 calories (7000 calories per week), weight loss is increased to about 2 pounds per week. It is important to note, however, that weight loss may vary slightly depending upon the particular individual. Two pounds per week is about the maximum weight loss most physicians recommend unless the individual is under a specific medically supervised program.

But it's not just simply a matter of consuming a set number of calories. You must, also, balance your diet nutritionally. To do this, each day's menus should provide the number of servings recommended by the Basic Four. To check this, use the Basic Four Menu Guide (see next page) for planning your menus. Select foods from each group which are relatively low in calories. However, if the daily caloric allotment is quite low, it is not always possible to include the total recommended number of servings from the Bread-Cereal Group in the Basic Four.

To plan a lunch or dinner menu, select a main dish from the Meat Group which provides one serving for each family member. (The breakfast menu may or may not include a main dish.) Add a vegetable, salad, bread, dessert, and beverage which complements the main dish in flavor, texture, and color. Avoid food preparation methods such as frying or sautéeing which tend to add calories. Instead, prepare food by broiling, roasting, poaching, or steaming. When possible, serve fruits and vegetables raw to keep calories low.

Use the calorie-counted menus (see pages 66-73) as a guide for planning your menus. Note that the breakfast menu often provides fewer calories than either lunch or dinner. However, this pattern can be adjusted, depending upon personal preference. Remember: serving portions must be controlled for an effective diet. A wider variety of foods which are nutritionally sound are possible when menus are planned in advance.

FIGURING CALORIC NEEDS

1. Estimate desirable weight for your height by consulting a weight chart.

2. Multiply your desirable weight by the number 16 if you are a woman and 18 if you are a man. (These numbers are based on a light amount of physical activity. Additional calories will be needed by those who regularly engage in strenuous physical activities. Since many people tend to overestimate their energy requirements, the above figures are a satisfactory guide for most people in their daily routine.)

3. Subtract 10 calories for each year of age over 22. (Desired weight at age 22 should be maintained throughout life. As you grow older, fewer calories are needed to maintain weight.)

BASIC FOUR MENU GUIDE

Milk Group—2 to 4 cups daily

Includes milk, buttermilk, yogurt, ice cream, and cheese.
    Recommended allowances:
        2 to 3 cups for children
        4 or more cups for teenagers
        2 or more cups for adults
    Calcium equivalents for 1 cup milk:
        1⅓ ounces Cheddar-type cheese
        1½ cups cottage cheese
        1 pint (2 cups) ice cream

Meat Group—2 servings daily

Includes beef, veal, pork, lamb, poultry, fish, and eggs. Alternate sources of protein include dry beans, dry peas, nuts, and peanut butter.
    Consider as one serving:
        2 to 3 ounces cooked meat, fish, or
            poultry
        2 eggs
        1 cup cooked dry beans, peas, or lentils
        4 tablespoons peanut butter

Vegetable-Fruit Group—4 servings daily

Include tomatoes or one serving of citrus fruit daily and one serving of a dark green leafy vegetable, deep yellow vegetable, or yellow fruit 3 to 4 times a week.
    Consider as one serving:
        ½ cup fruit or vegetable
        1 medium apple, banana, or potato
        ½ grapefruit or cantaloupe

Bread-Cereal Group—4 servings daily

Includes breads, cereals, cornmeal, grits, crackers, pasta, rice, and quick breads. These products should be made from whole grain, enriched, or restored cereals.
    Consider as one serving:
        1 slice bread
        ¾ to 1 cup ready-to-eat cereal
        ½ to ¾ cup cooked cereal, rice,
            macaroni, noodles, or spaghetti

1000 Calorie Menus

Day 1

BREAKFAST—206 calories
½ cup Orange Juice
½ cup fortified Crisp Rice Cereal
¼ cup Skim Milk   1 teaspoon Sugar
1 Boiled Egg
Coffee or Tea

LUNCH—306 calories
Salmon Sandwich*
1 cup Lettuce
1 tablespoon low-cal
Italian Salad Dressing
½ cup Green Grapes
¾ cup Skim Milk   Coffee or Tea

DINNER—498 calories
Liver with Mushrooms*
Sesame Broccoli*
Carrot-Orange Salad*
Pineapple-Mint Dessert*
1 cup Skim Milk   Coffee or Tea

Day 4

BREAKFAST—204 calories
½ cup Fresh Strawberries
1 cup Crisp Rice Cereal
½ cup Skim Milk   1 teaspoon Sugar
Coffee or Tea

LUNCH—360 calories
3 ounces lean Broiled Ground Beef Patty
½ Hamburger Bun
1 teaspoon Catsup or Mustard
1 cup Lettuce
1 tablespoon low-cal
Blue Cheese Salad Dressing
Lemon-Blueberry Fluff*
½ cup Skim Milk   Coffee or Tea

DINNER—448 calories
Seafood Divan*
½ cup Cottage Cheese
½ medium Fresh Peach on Lettuce Leaf
Grapefruit-Berry Compote*
1 cup Skim Milk   Coffee or Tea

Day 5

BREAKFAST—222 calories
½ cup Grapefruit Juice
½ cup Enriched Wheat Cereal
¼ cup Skim Milk   1 teaspoon Sugar
1 Soft-Cooked Egg
Coffee or Tea

LUNCH—275 calories
Shrimp-Stuffed Tomato*
Spicy Peach Compote*
1 cup Skim Milk   Coffee or Tea

DINNER—516 calories
Hawaiian Ham Slice*
½ small Baked Sweet Potato
Herbed Bean Salad*
Lime Snow*
¾ cup Skim Milk   Coffee or Tea

*These recipes are provided for you in the recipe section. See Index listing for page number.

Day 2

BREAKFAST—*236 calories*
1 medium Fresh Peach
1 cup Farina
½ cup Skim Milk   1 teaspoon Sugar
Coffee or Tea

LUNCH—*324 calories*
Super Chef Salad*
2 Melba Toast Rounds
Cranberry Sherbet*
½ cup Skim Milk   Coffee or Tea

DINNER—*447 calories*
Fruited Chicken Breasts*
½ cup Spinach
Dilly Tomato Slices*
1 slice Italian Bread
Rhubarb-Strawberry Bowl*
1 cup Skim Milk   Coffee or Tea

½ teaspoon butter or margarine
allowed for the day

Day 3

BREAKFAST—*220 calories*
¼ medium Cantaloupe
½ cup Puffed Wheat Cereal
⅓ cup Skim Milk   1 teaspoon Sugar
1 Oven-Baked Egg
Coffee or Tea

LUNCH—*278 calories*
Deluxe Crab Broil*
Baked Crimson Pear*
⅔ cup Skim Milk   Coffee or Tea

DINNER—*496 calories*
Pepper Steak*
½ cup Rice
1 cup Lettuce
1 tablespoon low-cal
French-Style Salad Dressing
½ cup Pineapple Chunks
1 cup Skim Milk   Coffee or Tea

½ teaspoon butter or margarine
allowed for the day

Day 6

BREAKFAST—*202 calories*
¾ cup Vegetable Juice Cocktail
½ cup Cornflakes
¼ cup Skim Milk   1 teaspoon Sugar
1 slice Cracked Wheat Toast
Coffee or Tea

LUNCH—*270 calories*
French Onion Soup*
Dieter's Tuna Salad*
2 Crisp Rye Crackers
¼ medium Cantaloupe
¾ cup Skim Milk   Coffee or Tea

DINNER—*522 calories*
Italian Veal Cutlet*
½ cup Asparagus
Pineapple Mold*
Raspberry-Yogurt Fuff*
1 cup Skim Milk   Coffee or Tea

1 teaspoon butter or margarine
allowed for the day

Day 7

BREAKFAST—*231 calories*
½ cup low-cal Cranberry Juice Cocktail
Mushroom Omelet*
1 slice Raisin Toast
Coffee or Tea

LUNCH—*270 calories*
Chicken-Romaine Salad*
Blueberry Ice*
1 cup Skim Milk   Coffee or Tea

DINNER—*507 calories*
½ cup Consommé
2 Saltine Crackers
Oven-Style Swiss Steak*
Broccoli Salad Bowl*
Honeydew-Berry Parfait*
1 cup Skim Milk   Coffee or Tea

½ teaspoon butter or margarine
allowed for the day

1200 Calorie Menus

Day 1

BREAKFAST—*230 calories*
½ Grapefruit
½ cup Puffed Wheat Cereal
½ cup Skim Milk   1 teaspoon Sugar
1 Poached Egg
Coffee or Tea

LUNCH—*384 calories*
Cottage-Shrimp Toss*
4 Crisp Rye Crackers
¼ medium Cantaloupe
1 cup Skim Milk   Coffee or Tea

DINNER—*578 calories*
Stuffed Cube Steak*
Baked-Stuffed Potato*
1 cup Lettuce   1 small Tomato
1 tablespoon low-cal
Italian Salad Dressing
Ambrosia*
1 cup Skim Milk   Coffee or Tea

Day 4

BREAKFAST—*219 calories*
1 small Banana
½ cup Bran Flakes
½ cup Skim Milk   1 teaspoon Sugar
Coffee or Tea

LUNCH—*381 calories*
Open-Face Beefburger*
Blueberry Ice*
1 cup Skim Milk   Coffee or Tea

DINNER—*612 calories*
Peach-Sauced Ham*
½ large Baked Sweet Potato
½ cup Green Beans
Orange Perfection Salad*
1 slice Whole Wheat Bread
Rhubarb-Strawberry Bowl*
½ cup Skim Milk   Coffee or Tea

1 teaspoon butter or margarine
allowed for the day

Day 5

BREAKFAST—*225 calories*
½ cup Tomato Juice
½ cup Oatmeal
¼ cup Skim Milk   2 teaspoons Sugar
1 slice Whole Wheat Toast
Coffee or Tea

LUNCH—*396 calories*
Hot Cheese Egg Sandwich*
½ cup Carrot and Celery Sticks
1 cup Lettuce
1 tablespoon low-cal Italian Salad Dressing
2 medium Fresh Apricots
1 cup Skim Milk   Coffee or Tea

DINNER—*579 calories*
Italian Sauced Fish*
½ cup Whipped Potatoes   ½ cup Wax Beans
Artichoke-Fruit Salad*
1 slice Italian Bread
Raspberry-Apple Dessert*
1 cup Skim Milk   Coffee or Tea

2 teaspoons butter or margarine
allowed for the day

*These recipes are provided for you in the recipe section. See Index listing for page number.

Day 2

BREAKFAST—*237 calories*
½ cup Orange Juice
1 Scrambled Egg
1 slice Cracked Wheat Toast
1 teaspoon low-cal Strawberry Jam
Coffee or Tea

LUNCH—*381 calories*
Ham-Asparagus Broil*
1 cup Lettuce
1 tablespoon low-cal
French-Style Salad Dressing
½ cup Green Grapes
1 cup Skim Milk   Coffee or Tea

DINNER—*575 calories*
London Broil*
Ruby-Sauced Beets*   Oriental Spinach*
1 slice Rye Bread
Mocha Chiffon*
1 cup Skim Milk   Coffee or Tea

2 teaspoons butter or margarine
allowed for the day

Day 3

BREAKFAST—*222 calories*
½ cup Apricot Nectar
1 Soft-Cooked Egg
1 slice Whole Wheat Toast
Coffee or Tea

LUNCH—*428 calories*
Chicken Open-Face*
⅓ cup Cottage Cheese
½ cup Carrot Sticks
1 medium Fresh Peach
1 cup Skim Milk   Coffee or Tea

DINNER—*569 calories*
Salmon Dolmas*
½ cup Peas
1 small Tomato
1 slice Italian Bread
Pineapple-Mint Dessert*
1 cup Skim Milk   Coffee or Tea

1½ teaspoons butter or margarine
allowed for the day

Day 6

BREAKFAST—*224 calories*
¼ medium Cantaloupe
1 Oven-Baked Egg
1 slice White Toast
Coffee or Tea

LUNCH—*362 calories*
Ham and Salad Roll*
2 medium Fresh Plums
1 cup Skim Milk   Coffee or Tea

DINNER—*615 calories*
Tomato-Sauced Chicken*
½ cup Parslied Potatoes
Sesame Broccoli*
½ cup Coleslaw
Marinated Fruit*
1 cup Skim Milk   Coffee or Tea

2½ teaspoons butter or margarine
allowed for the day

Day 7

BREAKFAST—*217 calories*
½ cup Grapefruit Juice
½ cup Whole Wheat Flakes
¼ cup Skim Milk   1 teaspoon Sugar
1 slice Whole Wheat Toast
Coffee or Tea

LUNCH—*391 calories*
Crab-Artichoke Toss*
2 Crisp Rye Crackers
½ cup Fresh Strawberries
2-inch slice Angel Food Cake
¾ cup Skim Milk   Coffee or Tea

DINNER—*596 calories*
¾ cup Vegetable Juice Cocktail
Marinated Pot Roast*
Turnip-Carrot Duo*
Blender Cucumber Salad*
Peachy Orange Ice*
1 cup Skim Milk   Coffee or Tea

½ teaspoon butter or margarine
allowed for the day

1500 Calorie Menus

Day 1

BREAKFAST—334 calories
1 small Orange
1 cup Oatmeal   2 teaspoons Sugar
1 cup Skim Milk   Coffee or Tea

LUNCH—514 calories
Salmon-Stuffed Tomato*
10 Potato Chips
½ cup Carrot Sticks
Snow Pudding*
½ cup Skim Milk   Coffee or Tea

DINNER—642 calories
3½ ounces Roast Beef
Baked-Stuffed Potato*
½ cup Beets
Sauerkraut Salad*
1 slice French Bread
½ cup Ice Milk
½ cup Fresh Strawberries
½ cup Skim Milk   Coffee or Tea

1½ teaspoons butter or margarine
allowed for the day

Day 4

BREAKFAST—409 calories
½ medium Cantaloupe
¾ cup Whole Bran Cereal
1½ teaspoons Sugar
1 Soft-Cooked Egg
1 cup Skim Milk   Coffee or Tea

LUNCH—460 calories
1 cup Tomato Soup   1 Cheese Sandwich
1 cup Lettuce
1 tablespoon low-cal Italian Salad Dressing
Apple-Ginger Bake*
Coffee or Tea

DINNER—638 calories
Orange-Halibut Fillet*
½ cup Mashed Potatoes
Saucy Brussels Sprouts*   Pineapple Mold*
2-inch square Corn Bread
Baked Crimson Pear*
1 cup Skim Milk   Coffee or Tea

1½ teaspoons butter or margarine
allowed for the day

Day 5

BREAKFAST—316 calories
½ cup Tomato Juice
1 poached Egg
1 slice Raisin Toast
1 cup Skim Milk   Coffee or Tea

LUNCH—467 calories
Peach and Chicken Cup*
½ cup Carrot Sticks
2 Crisp Rye Crackers
Rice Pudding Royale*
½ cup Skim Milk   Coffee or Tea

DINNER—709 calories
Pineapple-Pork Chop*
½ cup Whole Kernel Corn
Ruby Sauced Beets*
½ medium Fresh Pear on Lettuce Leaf
1 Hot Biscuit
Raspberry Bavarian Mold*
½ cup Skim Milk   Coffee or Tea

2½ teaspoons butter or margarine
allowed for the day

*These recipes are provided for you in the recipe section. See Index listing for page number.

Day 2

BREAKFAST—315 calories
¾ cup Vegetable Juice Cocktail
1 Scrambled Egg
1 slice White Toast
1 cup Skim Milk   Coffee or Tea

LUNCH—512 calories
Macaroni-Cheese Puff*
Carrot-Orange Salad*
1 medium Fresh Pear
1 cup Skim Milk   Coffee or Tea

DINNER—678 calories
3½ ounces Roast Loin of Pork
½ cup Parslied Potatoes
½ cup Italian Green Beans
Sunshine Apple Mold*
1 Plain Muffin
Grapefruit-Berry Compote*
Coffee or Tea

1 tablespoon butter or margarine
allowed for the day

Day 3

BREAKFAST—325 calories
½ cup Orange Juice
1 slice French Toast
1 tablespoon Maple Syrup
Coffee or Tea

LUNCH—507 calories
1 cup Cream of Celery Soup
Deviled Ham Burger*
Lemon-Blueberry Fluff*
¾ cup Skim Milk   Coffee or Tea

DINNER—679 calories
Barbecued Chuck Roast*
Onion-Potato Bake*
Basil Carrots*
1 cup Lettuce
1 tablespoon low-cal
Blue Cheese Salad Dressing
Ambrosia*
1 cup Skim Milk   Coffee or Tea

1½ teaspoons butter or margarine
allowed for the day

Day 6

BREAKFAST—334 calories
¼ medium Honeydew Melon
1 Blueberry Muffin
1 slice Broiled Bacon
1 cup Skim Milk   Coffee or Tea

LUNCH—541 calories
½ cup Creamed Chipped Beef on 1 Rusk
1 cup Lettuce   1 small Tomato
1 tablespoon low-cal
French-Style Salad Dressing
Baked Orange Cup*
1 cup Skim Milk   Coffee or Tea

DINNER—641 calories
Deviled Steak*
½ cup Scalloped Potatoes   ⅔ cup Broccoli
Blender Cucumber Salad*
1 slice French Bread
Lime Snow*   2 Vanilla Wafers
Coffee or Tea

2 teaspoons butter or margarine
allowed for the day

Day 7

BREAKFAST—347 calories
½ cup Grapefruit Juice
1 Oven-Baked Egg   2 slices Broiled Bacon
1 Yeast Doughnut
Coffee or Tea

LUNCH—558 calories
Chicken-Artichoke Bowl*
3 Bread Sticks
Cranberry Sherbet*
1 cup Skim Milk   Coffee or Tea

DINNER—596 calories
Mushroom Cocktail*
Broiled Beef Fillet*
1 medium Baked Potato
Cauliflower Italiano*
1 cup Lettuce
1 tablespoon low-cal
Blue Cheese Salad Dressing
Meringue-Topped Peach*
1 cup Skim Milk   Coffee or Tea

½ teaspoon butter or margarine
allowed for the day

1800 Calorie Menus

Day 1

BREAKFAST—392 calories
½ cup Grape Juice
¾ cup Oatmeal   1 teaspoon Sugar
1 slice White Toast
1 cup Skim Milk   Coffee or Tea

LUNCH—621 calories
Ham and Cheese Medley*
14 Potato Chips
Rice Pudding Royale*
1 cup Skim Milk   Coffee or Tea

DINNER—792 calories
Curried Chicken*
½ cup Mashed Potatoes
Peas with Mushrooms*
Sunshine Apple Mold*
1 Dinner Roll
½ medium Cantaloupe
⅓ cup Vanilla Ice Cream
Coffee or Tea

2½ teaspoons butter or margarine
allowed for the day

Day 4

BREAKFAST—386 calories
Grapefruit Half
1 Scrambled Egg
1 slice Broiled Bacon
1 slice Raisin Toast
1 cup Skim Milk   Coffee or Tea

LUNCH—549 calories
Swiss Cheese Soufflé*
Baked Deviled Tomato*
Yogurt Fruit Medley*   2 Vanilla Wafers
1 cup Skim Milk   Coffee or Tea

DINNER—858 calories
Onion Smothered Steak*
Vegetable Fiesta*
Broccoli Salad Bowl*
1 Hard Roll
⅓ cup Frozen Raspberries
2-inch slice Angel Food Cake
1 cup Skim Milk   Coffee or Tea

1 tablespoon butter or margarine
allowed for the day

Day 5

BREAKFAST—416 calories
¾ cup Vegetable Juice Cocktail
1 Oven-Baked Egg   1 slice Canadian Bacon
1 slice White Toast
1 cup Skim Milk   Coffee or Tea

LUNCH—547 calories
Tangy Seafood Toss*
3 Bread Sticks
Peachy Orange Ice*
1 cup Skim Milk   Coffee or Tea

DINNER—836 calories
Cranberry-Sauced Burger*
½ small Baked Acorn Squash
Skillet Onion Slices*
1 cup Lettuce
1 tablespoon low-cal
French-Style Salad Dressing
1 Dinner Roll
2-inch square Frosted Devil's Food Cake
1 cup Skim Milk   Coffee or Tea

4 teaspoons butter or margarine
allowed for the day

*These recipes are provided for you in the recipe section. See Index listing for page number.

Day 2

BREAKFAST—418 calories
½ cup Orange Juice
1 Poached Egg
1 Sweet Roll
½ cup Skim Milk   Coffee or Tea

LUNCH—514 calories
Shrimp Stack-Up*
½ cup Carrot Sticks
½ cup Vanilla Ice Cream
2 tablespoons Chocolate Sauce
1 cup Skim Milk   Coffee or Tea

DINNER—861 calories
Basic Meat Loaf*
½ cup Scalloped Potatoes
Herbed Tomato Half*
Artichoke-Fruit Salad*
1 Hot Biscuit
Honeydew-Berry Parfait*
1 cup Skim Milk   Coffee or Tea

1 tablespoon butter or margarine
allowed for the day

Day 3

BREAKFAST—404 calories
½ medium Cantaloupe
2 medium Pancakes
2 tablespoons Maple Syrup
Coffee or Tea

LUNCH—636 calories
Turkey Hawaiian*
Dilly Tomato Slices*
1 Whole Wheat Roll
Lime Snow*
1 cup Skim Milk   Coffee or Tea

DINNER—773 calories
Orange-Glazed Lamb*
Baked-Stuffed Potato*
Asparagus with Cheese*
1 cup Lettuce
1 tablespoon low-cal Russian Salad Dressing
1 slice Rye Bread
Fresh Peach Compote*
1 cup Skim Milk   Coffee or Tea

2 teaspoons butter or margarine
allowed for the day

Day 6

BREAKFAST—387 calories
1 medium Orange
¾ cup Farina   1 teaspoon Sugar
1 slice Whole Wheat Toast
1 cup Skim Milk   Coffee or Tea

LUNCH—571 calories
Frank-Kraut Skillet*
Sunshine Aspic*
1 slice Rye Bread
Glorified Rice*
1 cup Skim Milk   Coffee or Tea

DINNER—847 calories
Orange-Halibut Fillet*
1 small Baked Sweet Potato
Green Beans with Onions*
Raspberry-Cheese Mold*
1 Cornmeal Muffin
Apple-Ginger Bake*
1 cup Skim Milk   Coffee or Tea

3½ teaspoons butter or margarine
allowed for the day

Day 7

BREAKFAST—465 calories
½ cup Prune Juice
1 Scrambled Egg   1 Pork Sausage Link
1 slice Cracked Wheat Toast
1 cup Skim Milk   Coffee or Tea

LUNCH—563 calories
Deviled Ham Burger*
Asparagus Viniagrette*   ½ cup Carrot Sticks
Baked Orange Cup*
1 cup Skim Milk   Coffee or Tea

DINNER—772 calories
French Onion Soup*
Marinated Beef Kabobs*
1 medium Baked Potato
1 cup Lettuce
1 tablespoon low-cal Russian Salad Dressing
1 slice Italian Bread
Snow Pudding*
1 cup Skim Milk   Coffee or Tea

4 teaspoons butter or margarine
allowed for the day

Low-Calorie Entertaining

Have difficulty keeping the calories low when you entertain? Page through this section for party menus designed to flatter but not fatten. Whether it's a brunch, lunch, holiday dinner, or buffet, diet-conscious guests are sure to voice their approval—and non-dieters will never suspect you're keeping a tally on calories. Serve the food buffet-style and let guests help themselves—a very important consideration for calorie-watchers.

Entertain guests at a buffet featuring Shrimp Elegante, Fluffy Rice, Spinach-Artichoke Salad, French bread, and dessert.

WEEKEND BRUNCH

```
┌─────────────────────────────────┐
│            MENU                  │
│          448 calories            │
│                                  │
│    Two-Tone Juice Starter        │
│    Shirred Eggs Deluxe           │
│    Marmalade-Toast Strips        │
│    Melon Balls Melba             │
│          Coffee                  │
└─────────────────────────────────┘
```

TWO-TONE JUICE STARTER
50 calories / serving

A delightful two-colored, morning eye-opener—

- 1 12-ounce can apricot nectar, chilled (1½ cups)
- 1½ cups low-calorie cranberry juice cocktail

Into each of 6 glasses pour ¼ cup of the apricot nectar; then tip glass and very slowly pour ¼ cup of the cranberry juice cocktail down side of glass. Do not stir. Makes 6 servings.

SHIRRED EGGS DELUXE
252 calories / serving

Topped with mushrooms, bacon, and cheese—

- 2 tablespoons butter or margarine
- 12 eggs
  Dash salt
  Dash pepper
- ¾ cup sliced fresh mushrooms
- 6 slices bacon, crisp-cooked and crumbled
- ⅓ cup grated Parmesan cheese

Allowing *1 teaspoon* each, butter 6 shallow individual casseroles. Break two eggs into each casserole; add dash salt and pepper. Bake at 325° for 15 minutes. Top with mushrooms, crumbled bacon, and cheese; return eggs to oven and bake 5 minutes longer. Serves 6.

MARMALADE-TOAST STRIPS
83 calories / serving

Everyone gets four crusty toast strips bubbling with orange marmalade and flavored with cinnamon, hot from the oven—

- 6 slices white bread, lightly toasted
- ⅓ cup low-calorie orange marmalade
- 1 teaspoon ground cinnamon

Trim crusts from toast. Combine marmalade and cinnamon; spread on toast. Cut each slice in 4 strips. Broil 4 inches from heat till marmalade bubbles, about 1 minute. Makes 24 strips.

MELON BALLS MELBA
63 calories / serving

Serve the cranberry sauce over other melon and fresh fruit desserts—

- ½ cup low-calorie cranberry juice cocktail
- 1 teaspoon cornstarch
- 4 drops almond flavoring (optional)

• • •

- 1 cup fresh raspberries
- 1 tablespoon sugar
- 3 cups cantaloupe balls
  Mint sprigs

Gradually blend cranberry juice cocktail with cornstarch. Cook and stir over medium heat till mixture is thick and bubbly; remove from heat. Stir in almond flavoring. Cool.

Sprinkle fresh raspberries with sugar; spoon berries into sherbet glasses with cantaloupe balls. Spoon on cooled cranberry sauce. Garnish with mint sprigs. Makes 6 servings.

Refreshing brunch finale

Conclude the morning brunch with Melon → Balls Melba. Golden cantaloupe balls and red raspberries bask in cranberry sauce.

ENTERTAINING AT LUNCH

MENU
487 calories

Confetti Consommé
Hot Crunch Sticks
Corned Beef Roll-Ups
Mandarin-Pear Salad
Coffee Chiffon Torte
Coffee

CONFETTI CONSOMMÉ

22 calories / serving

Colorful vegetable flecks in a hot soup starter—

- 2 10½-ounce cans condensed chicken broth
- ½ cup shredded carrot
- ¼ cup finely chopped green pepper
- ¼ cup finely chopped green onion

In medium saucepan combine chicken broth, 1⅔ cups water, and vegetables. Heat to boiling. Serve hot. Makes 10 servings.

HOT CRUNCH STICKS

70 calories / serving

Each refrigerated biscuit makes two bread sticks—

- 1 cup crisp rice cereal, crushed slightly
- 1 tablespoon dill seed
- 1 teaspoon salt
- 1 package refrigerated biscuits (10 biscuits)

Mix cereal crumbs, seed, and salt in shallow pan (be sure salt is well distributed). Cut biscuits in half; roll each half into a pencil-thin stick, about 4 inches long. Brush with water. Roll sticks in mixture. Place on greased baking sheet. Bake at 450° till sticks are lightly browned, about 10 minutes. Serve sticks warm. Makes 20.

MANDARIN-PEAR SALAD

143 calories / serving

Blue cheese dressing complements fresh pears—

- 1 8-ounce carton yogurt
- 2 tablespoons sugar
- 2 tablespoons blue cheese, crumbled
  . . .
- 5 fresh medium pears, unpeeled, cored, and halved
  Leaf lettuce
- 2 11-ounce cans mandarin orange sections, chilled and drained

In small mixer bowl, combine yogurt, sugar, and *1 tablespoon* of the crumbled blue cheese. Beat dressing mixture with rotary beater or electric mixer till smooth. Sprinkle dressing with remaining crumbled blue cheese.

Arrange pear halves on lettuce. Fill centers with mandarin orange sections. Pass blue cheese dressing. Makes 10 servings.

Serve molded Coffee Chiffon Torte—a delectable dessert dusted with gingersnap crumbs and topped with creamy topping.

CORNED BEEF ROLL-UPS

121 calories / serving

Dill pickle chunk tops each meat roll—

Using 1¼ pounds thinly sliced corned beef, roll each slice jelly-roll fashion. Slice 2 or 3 whole dill pickles into ½ inch chunks. Place dill pickle slice on end of wooden pick; insert in corned beef roll-up. Makes 10 servings.

COFFEE CHIFFON TORTE

121 calories / serving

Only looks like a calorie dessert splurging—

     2 envelopes unflavored gelatin
        (2 tablespoons)
   ½ cup cold water
  2½ cups skim milk
     3 egg yolks
   ½ cup sugar
     1 teaspoon salt
     4 teaspoons instant coffee powder
          • • •
     3 egg whites
     1 teaspoon vanilla
   ¼ teaspoon cream of tartar
     4 gingersnaps, crushed
   ⅔ cup frozen whipped dessert topping,
        thawed

Soften gelatin in cold water. Beat together milk and egg yolks. Add sugar, salt, coffee powder, and softened gelatin. Cook, stirring constantly, till gelatin dissolves and mixture is thick and bubbly. Chill till partially set.

Beat together egg whites, vanilla, and cream of tartar till soft peaks form. Fold in gelatin mixture. Chill till mixture mounds. Spoon into 6½-cup mold. Chill till firm.

At serving time, unmold and sprinkle with *half* of the gingersnap crumbs. Spoon on thawed whipped topping; garnish with remaining gingersnap crumbs. Makes 10 servings.

Buffet-style luncheon

All your friends will want to be luncheon guests when you serve Mandarin-Pear Salad with dressing and Corned Beef Roll-Ups.

FAMILY HOLIDAY DINNER

HOLIDAY COCKTAIL DELUXE

67 calories / serving

Begin festivities with this chilled appetizer—

4 white grapefruit, sectioned
⅓ cup pomegranate seeds
1 tablespoon grenadine syrup
1 cup low-calorie lemon-lime
    carbonated beverage, chilled

In bowl combine grapefruit sections, pomegranate seeds and grenadine syrup. Chill at least 30 minutes, stirring once or twice.

To serve, spoon fruit and syrup into sherbet dishes. Slowly pour lemon-lime carbonated beverage over fruit mixture. Makes 8 servings.

HERBED PEAS AND ONIONS

32 calories / serving

Lightly flavored with lemon juice and basil—

2 cups frozen peas
1 8-ounce can peeled small whole
    stewed onions, drained
1 tablespoon lemon juice
½ teaspoon dried basil leaves, crushed

Cook peas according to package directions; do not drain. Add canned onions; heat through. Drain thoroughly. Combine lemon juice and crushed basil; pour over peas and onions. Toss lightly to coat vegetables. Makes 8 servings.

ROAST TURKEY

176 calories / serving

Each dieter gets 3½-ounces of light meat—

Rinse and pat dry one 6- to 8-pound turkey. Sprinkle inside with salt; truss. Place, breast side up, on rack in shallow roasting pan. Lightly rub skin with salad oil. Insert meat thermometer, without touching bone, in center of inside thigh muscle. Top loosely with foil. Press down lightly at end of drumsticks and neck, leaving air space between bird and foil.

Bake at 325° till done, about 3½ to 4 hours. During last 45 minutes of roasting, remove turkey from oven and cut band of skin or string between legs and tail; continue roasting, uncovered, till turkey is tender. (When done, the drumstick moves up and down and twists easily in socket. Meat thermometer should register 185°.) Remove bird from oven; let stand 15 minutes before carving. Makes 8 servings.

RICE DRESSING

34 calories / serving

Flavorful rice dish complements holiday turkey—

½ cup uncooked long-grain rice
½ cup chopped celery
¼ cup chopped onion
3 chicken bouillon cubes
1 16-ounce can bean sprouts,
    drained and rinsed
1 4-ounce can sliced mushrooms,
    drained
½ teaspoon poultry seasoning
⅛ teaspoon rubbed sage
    Dash pepper

In saucepan combine rice, celery, onion, bouillon cubes, ¼ teaspoon salt, and 1½ cups water. Bring to boiling; reduce heat. Simmer, covered, till rice is tender, about 20 minutes.

Remove from heat; stir in remaining ingredients and ⅓ cup water. Turn into 1-quart casserole. Bake, covered, at 350° till heated through, about 30 minutes. Makes 8 servings.

CRAN-ORANGE SALAD

64 calories / serving

Sparkling clear red ring with crisp celery and orange pieces inside the gelatin—

In small saucepan soften 2 envelopes unflavored gelatin (2 tablespoons) in ½ cup low-calorie cranberry juice cocktail. Stir over low heat till gelatin is dissolved. Stir in additional 3½ cups low-calorie cranberry juice cocktail and ½ teaspoon grated orange peel; chill in the refrigerator till cranberry mixture is partially set.

Peel, seed, and dice 4 small oranges (about 2 cups). Fold in diced orange and ½ cup diced celery. Turn mixture into 5½- or 6½-cup mold. Chill till firm. Makes 8 servings.

PINEAPPLE FLUFF

73 calories / serving

A light and satisfying dessert with small pieces of refreshing pineapple scattered throughout—

        1   20-ounce can crushed pineapple
                (juice pack)
        1   envelope unflavored gelatin
                (1 tablespoon)
      ¼   cup sugar
        2   unbeaten egg whites
        3   to 4 drops yellow food coloring

Drain pineapple, reserving juice; add water to reserved pineapple juice to make 1½ cups. In medium saucepan combine gelatin, sugar, and ¼ teaspoon salt; add the reserved pineapple juice mixture. Stir over low heat till gelatin and sugar dissolve. Remove from heat; chill in the refrigerator till mixture is partially set.

Turn into large mixer bowl; add egg whites and yellow food coloring. Beat at high speed with electric mixer till light and fluffy, about 5 minutes. Fold in pineapple and chill again till partially set. Turn into 5½-cup mold; chill till firm. Unmold to serve. Makes 8 servings.

Turkey is on the table

Begin the feasting with the serving of the golden Roast Turkey. Calorie watcher's should choose the luscious light meat.

EVENING BUFFET

MENU
547 calories

Hot Tomato Refresher
Shrimp Elegante
Fluffy Rice
Spinach-Artichoke Salad
French Bread　　　Butter
Fruit Melange
Coffee or Tea

HOT TOMATO REFRESHER
35 calories / serving

Ideal as a help-yourself appetizer—

In large saucepan combine two 24-ounce cans vegetable juice cocktail, 2 tablespoons lemon juice, 2 teaspoons Worcestershire sauce, and ½ teaspoon ground allspice; heat through. Just before serving, float thin lemon slices atop hot beverage, if desired. Makes 12 servings.

SPINACH-ARTICHOKE SALAD
78 calories / serving

A quick-made, sophisticated salad—

    2 14-ounce cans artichoke hearts,
        drained
    1 cup low-calorie Italian salad
        dressing
    3 hard-cooked eggs
    6 cups torn fresh spinach
    6 cups torn lettuce

Halve artichoke hearts; marinate in Italian salad dressing for 1 hour in the refrigerator. Drain hearts, reserving dressing. Dice *2* of the hard-cooked eggs; sprinkle with salt.

In large salad bowl place spinach, lettuce, drained artichoke hearts, and diced eggs; toss lightly with reserved salad dressing. Slice remaining egg; arrange over salad. Serves 12.

SHRIMP ELEGANTE
152 calories / serving

Colorful combo of shrimp, Chinese pea pods, and tomatoes dressed in a glistening sauce—

    3 pounds fresh or frozen shrimp
        in shells (50 large)
    2 7-ounce packages frozen Chinese
        pea pods
    3 chicken bouillon cubes
    ½ cup chopped green onion
    3 tablespoons soy sauce
    1 teaspoon salt
    4 tablespoons cornstarch
    ¼ cup cold water
    4 medium tomatoes, cut into eighths

Thaw shrimp, if frozen; peel and devein. Set aside. Pour boiling water over pea pods and carefully break apart with fork; drain immediately. In large saucepan or Dutch oven dissolve bouillon cubes in 2½ cups boiling water; add shrimp, onion, soy sauce, and salt. Return to boiling; cook, uncovered, for 3 minutes, stirring the shrimp mixture occasionally.

Blend together cornstarch and cold water; stir into shrimp mixture. Cook, stirring constantly, till mixture thickens and bubbles. Add tomato wedges and drained pea pods. Cook till tomatoes are heated through, about 3 minutes longer. Makes 12 servings.

FLUFFY RICE
93 calories / serving

Spoon saucy shrimp mixture over hot rice—

In large saucepan combine 2 cups uncooked long-grain rice, 4 cups cold water, and 1 teaspoon salt; cover tightly. Bring to a vigorous boil, then turn heat low. Continue cooking 14 minutes (do not lift cover). Remove from heat; let rice stand, covered, for 10 minutes. (To test for doneness: Pinch grain of rice between thumb and forefinger. When no hard core remains, rice is done.) Garnish cooked rice with parsley sprigs. Makes 12 servings.

FRUIT MELANGE
87 calories / serving

Drizzle orange marmalade sauce flavored with candied ginger over fruit before serving—

1 16-ounce can pitted dark sweet
   cherries (water pack), drained
   and halved
1 pint fresh strawberries, sliced
   (2½ cups)
1 medium cantaloupe, cut into balls
   (about 2½ cups)
1 15¼-ounce can pineapple chunks
   (juice pack), drained

½ cup low-calorie orange marmalade
¼ cup hot water
1 teaspoon finely chopped
   candied ginger
1 medium-large banana, sliced (1 cup)
   Fresh mint

Chill fruits; layer cherries, strawberries, melon, and pineapple in compote or large glass bowl. Combine orange marmalade, hot water, and candied ginger. Drizzle over fruit. Chill.

Arrange banana atop fruit mixture. (To keep banana from darkening, dip in ascorbic acid color keeper or lemon juice mixed with a little water.) Garnish with mint. Serves 12.

Select your prettiest glass serving compote to serve elegant Fruit Melange. Combine and chill the colorful array of fresh and canned fruits in the compote before guests arrive.

Maintaining Your Weight

Are you the only family member
who has to count calories?
Then check this section for ways to
simplify meal preparation with
you and the family in mind.
Likewise, note the importance of
balancing your calorie intake with
your physical activities.
For further help, use the handy
clip-out calorie and cholesterol guide
to count calories when you're
away from home — whether
it's eating out, packing a lunch, or
attending a cocktail party.

**Plump, juicy fruit lends itself to
many uses served alone or
in combination with other foods
in a well-balanced diet.**

WHEN ONLY ONE FAMILY MEMBER DIETS

DIETER'S MENU
Dinner—507 calories

½ cup Consommé
2 Saltine Crackers
Oven-Style Swiss Steak*
Broccoli Salad Bowl*
Honeydew-Berry Parfait*
1 cup Skim Milk   Coffee or Tea

*See Index for recipe listing.

FAMILY MENU
Dinner—896 calories

½ cup Consommé
2 Saltine Crackers
Oven-Style Swiss Steak*
1 medium Baked Potato   1½ teaspoons Butter
½ cup Cooked Carrots   ½ teaspoon Butter
Broccoli Salad Bowl*
1 Hot Roll   1 teaspoon Butter
Honeydew-Berry Parfait*
1 cup Whole Milk   Coffee or Tea

One of the most difficult tasks in dieting is accepting the fact that you're often in the minority. The other battles in your pursuit to achieve a new figure are more easily overcome once you've established the importance of "doing it alone." Consider yourself fortunate if you have family members or friends who seek to encourage you as you travel down the path to slimness.

Your first step is to determine those foods you can eat that fit into your category of food likes. For the adage that "everything I like is either expensive or fattening" is more dependent upon personal habit than fact, and is rarely based on nutrient or caloric value. Once on your way you will soon discover that flavor is not necessarily sacrificed when low-calorie foods are prepared correctly.

Then you must learn to discipline your eating habits. If the housewife is on a diet, the discipline is easier than if another member of the family is involved. But eating with other family members is simplified when menus are planned with both dieters and non-dieters in mind. It isn't necessary to plan two entirely different menus. Instead, plan menus that are adjustable to allow more calories for non-dieters. Adding higher calorie foods, which are often restricted on the dieter's menu, is an easy way to provide more calories for other family members. Such foods as starchy vegetables, breads, fats, whole milk or whole milk products, and rich desserts are simple ways to increase calories for the non-dieter. (Note the menu above which has been increased by almost 400 calories.)

Food preparation methods need only a slight adjustment when one member of the family is dieting. For example, if vegetables are seasoned with butter or margarine, remove the dieter's serving from the pan before adding the butter or margarine. Or, if food is prepared with a sauce or gravy, pass the sauce or gravy at the table and allow each family member to serve himself. For salads, offer low-calorie salad dressings along with regular salad dressings.

The size of the serving is vitally important. Don't fall into the easy trap of selecting foods that only allow the dieter a very small serving. Avoid tempting the calorie counter by selecting foods which are low enough in calories to allow an adequate-sized serving. A well-planned menu provides a feeling of satisfaction and enjoyment for both dieters and non-dieters at the end of the meal. It meets the nutritional recommendations without going over the calorie allowance for each dieter.

WHEN YOU EAT OUT

The temptations for ignoring your diet are often greatest when eating out. Unfortunately, the silent, tell-tale calorie is disguised in many forms. The successful dieter, however, quickly learns how to avoid the pitfalls of eating out without announcing his predicament to those around him.

Lunch is undoubtedly the meal most often eaten away from home. If you carry your lunch, choose a low-calorie soup and/or sandwich and include plenty of fruits and vegetables. Reduce sandwich calories by packing foods which are easily assembled at mealtime for an open-face sandwich. To make your lunch seem larger, pack small amounts of several foods rather than generous portions of only one or two foods.

Eating out may also include dining in the home of friends. You can graciously control calories at such occasions without hampering the hostess or other guests. Count your blessings along with calories if the meal is served buffet-style. Take larger servings or seconds when low-calorie vegetables are offered. Don't hesitate to leave calories on your plate —trimmed-meat fat, rich sauces, gravies, breaded coatings, meat or poultry stuffings, and excess salad dressings or oils.

Likewise, you can master calories when eating in a restaurant. Most restaurant menus offer a wide selection of low-calorie foods for the discriminating calorie counter. Avoid foods that are fried or served in a rich sauce or gravy. Request a low-calorie salad dressing or sprinkle your salad with vinegar or lemon juice. Cut additional calories from your meal by omitting bread, crackers, butter or margarine, and rich desserts.

A cocktail party may present further temptations for the weight watcher. Although the cocktail hour is hardly a dieter's "cup of tea," it can occasionally be enjoyed even though you are counting calories. Learn to sip your drink slowly, avoiding the need for a refill. Remember—alcohol calories must be *added* to your calorie allowance and should not be used as a substitute for food. If you can't resist the hors d'oeuvres, limit yourself to a few at the beginning of the party and don't return for seconds.

ALCOHOLIC BEVERAGE CHART

The calorie counts for cocktails and mixed drinks are an average value for recipes prepared from standard guides published for bartenders. If other ingredients, such as ginger ale or fruit juices are used, the caloric value of these ingredients must be added. Because the choice of these added ingredients varies with individual taste, the following calorie counts for alcoholic beverages are only approximate.

Beer, 1 12-ounce can...171 calories
Champagne, 1 wine glass (4 ounces)..............................84 calories
Crème de menthe, 1 cordial glass.................................67 calories
Daiquiri, 1 cocktail glass...122 calories
Highball, 1 glass (8 ounces).......................................166 calories
Manhattan, 1 cocktail (3½ ounces)...............................164 calories
Martini, 1 cocktail (3½ ounces)...................................140 calories
Muscatel or Port, 1 wine glass (3½ ounces)......................158 calories
Old Fashioned, 1 glass (4 ounces)................................179 calories
Sauterne, California, 1 wine glass (3½ ounces)...................84 calories
Tom Collins, 1 tall glass (10 ounces)............................180 calories

EXERCISE AIDS WEIGHT LOSS

A slim, trim figure is generally the result of maintaining a balance between your physical activities and the amount of food you eat. Food habits change as you grow from infancy to adulthood; likewise, physical activities must change if you want to avoid the accumulation of pounds with the years.

Since the daily routine is somewhat controlled for most individuals, leisure time presents the greatest opportunity for developing a physical exercise program. A short, but regular physical activity period increases calorie expenditure as well as produces a noticeable improvement in muscle tone. If you tend to shy away from formal exercising, try shifting your view of sports from spectator to participant. Make exercise a habit in your life by engaging in physical activities which you enjoy. Whether it's walking, jogging, hiking, bicycling, swimming, golfing, dancing, or any other favorite sport, it's an excellent way to use calories and what's more—it keeps you away from the refrigerator.

Long hours of strenuous activity are more tiresome and less effective in helping you maintain your weight than regular, less strenuous exercise. As you establish new eating habits, learn to develop a variety of physical activities which you will enjoy and which will become a part of your daily life.

PHYSICAL ACTIVITY CHART

Energy in the form of calories is required by the body to maintain body functions and to perform various physical activities. The number of calories needed is influenced by body composition, size, and age. The figures below, which include the calories needed for normal body functions, represent an approximate calorie need per hour. A calorie range for each group of activities is given to allow for individual body differences as well as for differences in the way each activity is performed. The higher values more closely correspond to the calorie needs for men, while the lower values more nearly represent the calorie requirements for women.

Sedentary Activities—80 to 100 calories per hour
   reading, writing, eating, watching television or movies, listening to the radio, sewing, playing cards, typing, miscellaneous light officework

Light Activities—110 to 160 calories per hour
   preparing food, washing dishes, dusting, light hand laundry, ironing, walking slowly, personal care, officework done while standing, rapid typing

Moderate Activities—170 to 240 calories per hour
   making beds, mopping and scrubbing, sweeping, light polishing and waxing, machine laundering, light gardening and carpentry work, walking moderately fast

Vigorous Activities—250 to 350 calories per hour
   heavy scrubbing and waxing, heavy hand laundry, hanging out clothes, stripping beds, walking fast, bowling, golfing, gardening

Strenuous Activities—350 or more calories per hour
   swimming, playing tennis, running, bicycling, dancing, skiing, playing football

CHOLESTEROL CHART

Cholesterol is present in all animal cells and is found in foods which are of animal origin. The cholesterol that appears in the food we eat is known as dietary cholesterol. The human body also manufactures cholesterol which is called body cholesterol.

Although scientific research continues into the role of cholesterol in the body, the relationship between dietary cholesterol and body cholesterol is still not clearly defined.

Foods useful in low cholesterol diets include lean meat, lean fish, vegetables, fruits, breads, cereals, margarine, vegetable oils, cottage cheese, buttermilk, skim or non-fat milk, and skim milk products. The following chart lists the amount of dietary cholesterol, in milligrams, which some of the more common foods contribute to the diet. The figures are based on a 100 gram serving (3½ ounces) of each food.

FOOD	CHOLESTEROL Milligrams per 100 grams
Beef, raw	70
Brains, raw	2000
Butter	250
Caviar or fish roe	300
Cheese	
Cheddar	100
Cottage, creamed	15
Cream	120
Other (25 to 30% fat)	85
Cheese spread	65
Chicken, flesh only, raw	60
Crab	125
Egg, whole	550
Egg white	0
Egg yolk	
Fresh	1500
Frozen	1280
Dried	2950
Fish	70
Heart, raw	150

FOOD	CHOLESTEROL Milligrams per 100 grams
Ice Cream	45
Kidney, raw	375
Lamb, raw	70
Lard and other animal fat	95
Liver, raw	300
Lobster	200
Margarine	
All vegetable fat	0
Two-thirds animal fat and one-third vegetable fat	65
Milk	
Fluid, whole	11
Dried, whole	85
Fluid, skim	3
Mutton	65
Oysters	200
Pork	70
Shrimp	125
Sweetbreads	250
Veal	90

CALORIE CHART

A

	Calories
Anchovy, canned, 3 thin fillets	21
Apple	
Baked, sweetened, 1 medium	188
Fresh, 1 medium	70
Juice, canned, 1 cup	116
Apple brown betty, ½ cup	170
Applesauce, canned	
Sweetened, ½ cup	115
Unsweetened, ½ cup	50
Apricots	
Canned, ½ cup in syrup	110
Dried, cooked, unsweetened, ½ cup in juice	120
Fresh, 2 to 3 medium	51
Nectar, 1 cup	140
Arrowroot, 1 tablespoon	29
Asparagus	
Canned, spears, green, medium, 6 spears	21
Canned, spears, white, medium, 6 spears	21
Cooked, ½ cup cut spears	15
Frozen, 6 spears	23
Avocado, peeled, ½	167

B

	Calories
Bacon, 2 crisp strips	96
Bacon, Canadian, 3 slices	195
Banana, 1 medium	85
Beans	
Baked, with tomato sauce and pork, ½ cup	160
Green, snap, fresh, ½ cup	15
Green, snap, frozen, 3½ ounces	25
Lima, cooked, ½ cup	130
Red kidney, canned or cooked, ½ cup	115
Yellow or wax, cooked, ½ cup	11
Beef cuts, cooked	
Corned, canned, 3 ounces	185
Hamburger, 3 ounce patty	
Lean ground beef (4 ounces uncooked)	185
Regular ground beef (4 ounces uncooked)	245

	Calories
Beef cuts, cooked, cont.	
Pot roast	
Lean and fat, 3 ounces	245
Lean only, 2½ ounces	140
Rib roast	
Lean and fat, 3 ounces	375
Lean only, 2 ounces	140
Round steak, 3 ounces	220
Sirloin steak, broiled, 3 ounces	330
Beef, dried, chipped, 2 ounces	115
Beef liver, fried, 2 ounces	130
Beef tongue, braised, 2 ounces	210
Beets, cooked, diced, ½ cup	27
Biscuit, baking powder, 1 (2½-inch diameter)	140
Blackberries, fresh, ½ cup	40
Blueberries, fresh, ½ cup	40
Bouillon cube, 1 cube	5
Bread	
Boston brown, 1 slice (3x¾ inch)	93
Corn, 1 piece (2-inch square)	93
French or Vienna, 1 slice	58
Italian, 1 slice	55
Raisin, 1 slice	60
Rye, 1 slice	56
White, 1 slice	62
Whole wheat, 1 slice	56
Broccoli, spears, cooked, ½ cup	20
Brussels sprouts, cooked, ½ cup	28
Butter, 1 tablespoon	100

C

	Calories
Cabbage, cooked, ½ cup	20
Cabbage, raw, red, shredded, 1 cup	31
Cabbage, raw, shredded, 1 cup	20
Cake	
Angel, 1/12 cake	135
Chocolate, 2 layers, chocolate icing, 2-inch wedge	445
Fruitcake	
Dark, 1 slice (3x3x½ inch)	152
Light, 1 slice (3x3x½ inch)	156

Cake, *cont.*

	Calories
Gingerbread, 2x2x2 inches	175
Pound, 1 slice (3x3x1½ inch)	142
Sponge, no icing, 1/10 cake	149
White, chocolate icing, 1 piece	226
White, no icing, 1 piece	188
Candy	
Caramel, 1 ounce (3 medium)	115
Chocolate creams, 1 ounce (2 to 3 pieces)	125
Chocolate, milk, 1 ounce bar	150
Chocolate, mints, 1 ounce (1 to 2 mints)	115
Gumdrops, 1 ounce (2½ large or 20 small)	100
Jelly beans, 1 ounce (10 beans)	105
Peanut brittle, 1 piece (2½x2x1¼x⅜ inch)	120
Cantaloupe, ¼ (5-inch diameter)	30
Carrots	
Cooked, diced, ½ cup	20
Raw, 1 large or 2 small	42
Catsup, 1 tablespoon	18
Cauliflower	
Cooked, flowerets, ½ cup	10
Raw, flowerets, 1 cup	27
Celery, raw, 2 stalks (8 inches long)	10
Cereal, cooked	
Cream of wheat, regular, ¾ cup	99
Oatmeal, ¾ cup	100
Wheat, rolled, ¾ cup	130
Cereal, ready-to-eat	
Bran flakes, ¾ cup	72
Cornflakes, ¾ cup	100
Oats, puffed, ¾ cup	78
Rice, puffed, ¾ cup	39
Wheat, flakes, ¾ cup	93
Wheat, puffed, ¾ cup	33
Wheat, shredded, 1 biscuit	100
Chard, cooked, ½ cup	15
Cheese	
American, process, 1 ounce	105
Blue, 1 ounce	103
Brick, 1 ounce	103
Camembert, 1 ounce	84
Cheddar, 1 ounce	112

Cheese, *cont.*

	Calories
Cottage, from skim milk, cream-style, 1 cup	239
Cottage, not creamed, 1 cup	200
Cream cheese, 1 ounce	105
Edam, 1 ounce	87
Gruyère, 1 ounce	115
Parmesan, grated, 3 tablespoons	60
Roquefort, 1 ounce	111
Soufflé, home recipe, 3½ ounces	218
Spread, American, 1 ounce	81
Swiss, 1 ounce	105
Cherries	
Canned (heavy syrup), tart or sweet, ½ cup	89
Canned (water pack), tart or sweet, red, ½ cup	43
Fresh, sweet, ½ cup	40
Chicken	
À la King, cooked, 3½ ounces	191
Chow mein, 3½ ounces	102
Fricassee, 3½ ounces	161
Fried, bone removed	
Dark meat, skinned, 3½ ounces	220
Dark meat, with skin, 3½ ounces	263
Light meat, skinned, 3½ ounces	197
Light meat, with skin, 3½ ounces	234
Potpie, 1 individual (4½-inch diameter)	535
Roasted, bone removed	
Dark meat, skinned, 3½ ounces	176
Light meat, skinned, 3½ ounces	176
Chili con carne with beans, canned, ½ cup	166
Chili sauce, 1 tablespoon	17
Chives, raw, chopped, 1 tablespoon	3
Chocolate	
Bitter, 1 square	142
Sweet, plain, 1 square	133
Syrup, thin-type, 1 tablespoon	50

Sandwich, 1 slice white bread, *cont.*

	Calories
Roast pork, hot, with 3 tablespoons gravy	503
Tuna salad	278
Sauerkraut, canned, ½ cup	20
Scallops, cooked, 3½ ounces	112
Sherbet, orange, ½ cup	130
Shortening, all-purpose, 1 tablespoon	125
Shrimp, canned, 3 ounces	100
Shrimp, French-fried, 3 ounces	191
Soup, condensed, diluted with water unless specified otherwise	
Canned	
Bean with pork, 1 cup	170
Beef bouillon, broth, consommé, 1 cup	30
Beef noodle, 1 cup	70
Chicken noodle, 1 cup	65
Clam chowder, Manhattan-style, 1 cup	85
Cream of asparagus, diluted with milk, 1 cup	140
Cream of celery, diluted with milk, 1 cup	166
Cream of mushroom, diluted with milk, 1 cup	211
Split-pea, 1 cup	145
Tomato, 1 cup	90
Vegetable with beef broth, 1 cup	80
Frozen	
Clam chowder, 1 serving	173
Cream of potato, 1 serving	87
Cream of shrimp, 1 serving	162
Green pea with ham, 1 serving	99
Oyster stew, 1 serving	133
Vegetable beef, 1 serving	67
Soy sauce, 1 tablespoon	8
Spaghetti, cooked, ½ cup	83
Spaghetti with meatballs in tomato sauce, home recipe, 1 cup	335
Spanish rice, home recipe, 1 cup	130
Spinach	
Canned, ½ cup	22
Frozen, chopped, cooked, ½ cup	23

Spinach, *cont.*

	Calories
Raw, 3½ ounces	26
Squash	
Summer, cooked, diced, ½ cup	15
Winter, baked, mashed, ½ cup	65
Strawberries	
Fresh, ½ cup	28
Frozen, sweetened, ½ cup	140
Sugar	
Brown, firm-packed, 1 tablespoon	50
Confectioners', 1 tablespoon	30
Granulated, 1 tablespoon	45

T-Z

	Calories
Tangerine, 1 medium	40
Tangerine juice, canned, ½ cup	100
Tapioca, granulated, 1 tablespoon	36
Tartar sauce, 1 tablespoon	95
Tomato paste, canned, 3½ ounces	82
Tomatoes	
Canned, ½ cup	25
Fresh, 1 medium	35
Juice, canned, 1 cup	40
Turkey, roasted, 3 slices (3x2½x2x¼ inch)	200
Turnip greens, cooked, ½ cup	15
Turnips, cooked, diced, ½ cup	20
Veal, cooked	
Cutlet, 3½ ounces	202
Loin chop, 3½ ounces	207
Sirloin roast, 3½ ounces	176
Vegetable juice cocktail, 1 cup	40
Vinegar, 1 tablespoon	2
Waffle, 1 (5½x4½x½ inch)	210
Water chestnuts, 4	20
Watercress, raw, 3½ ounces	19
Watermelon, 4x8-inch wedge	115
Welsh Rarebit, 3½ ounces	179
White sauce, medium, ½ cup	215
Yogurt	
Fruit-flavored, ½ cup	135
Plain, made from skim milk, ½ cup	61
Plain, made from whole milk, ½ cup	76
Zwieback, 1 piece	31

Cream
Half-and-half, 1 tablespoon ... 20
Heavy or whipping, 1 tablespoon ... 55
Light, 1 tablespoon ... 30
Whipped, unsweetened, 1 tablespoon ... 28
Cucumber, 6 slices (2x⅛ inch) ... 5
Custard, baked, ½ cup ... 140

D-F
Dates, fresh and dried, pitted, 1 cup ... 490
Doughnut
Cake type, plain, 1 ... 125
Sugar, icing, 1 ... 151
Yeast type, 1 ... 124
Jelly center, 1 ... 226
Egg
Fried, 1 large ... 100
Omelet, plain, 1 large egg ... 110
Poached, hard or soft-cooked, 1 large ... 82
Scrambled with milk and butter, 1 ... 110
White only, medium, 1 white ... 16
Whole, large, 1 ... 88
Whole, medium, 1 ... 78
Yolk only, medium, 1 ... 59
Eggplant
Cooked, drained, diced, ½ cup ... 19
Raw, diced, ½ cup ... 25
Endive, raw, 20 long leaves ... 20
Escarole, 4 large leaves ... 20
Figs
Canned, with syrup, ½ cup ... 110
Dried, 1 large ... 60
Raw, 3 small ... 90
Fish
Bass, baked, 3 ounces ... 216
Haddock, fried, 3 ounces ... 144
Halibut, broiled, 3 ounces ... 155
Ocean perch, fried, 3 ounces ... 195
Salmon
Broiled or baked, 3 ounces ... 154
Canned, pink, ½ cup ... 188
Canned, red, ½ cup ... 215
Loaf, 1 serving ... 122

Chop suey, with meat, 3½ ounces ... 120
Clam
Canned, ½ cup in liquor ... 52
Chowder
Manhattan, 1 serving ... 153
New England, 1 serving ... 259
Cocoa, (whole milk), 1 cup ... 235
Cocoa powder, unsweetened, 1 tablespoon ... 21
Coconut, shredded, dried, 2 tablespoons ... 83
Coffee or tea ... 0
Cola, carbonated beverage, 1 cup ... 95
Coleslaw, no lettuce, ⅔ cup ... 68
Collards, cooked, ½ cup ... 30
Cookie
Butter thin (2½-inch diameter) ... 50
Chocolate chip, 1 ... 52
Gingersnap, 1 ... 17
Sugar (3-inch diameter) ... 89
Vanilla wafer, 3 ... 51
Corn
Canned, whole kernel, ½ cup ... 85
Fritters, 3½ ounces ... 377
Sweet, cooked, 1 ear (5x1¾ inches) ... 70
Corn syrup, 1 tablespoon ... 60
Cornstarch, 1 tablespoon ... 29
Crab
Cakes, 1 serving ... 110
Imperial, 1 serving ... 235
Meat, canned, flaked, ½ cup ... 85
Crackers
Cheddar cheese, 10 small ... 20
Cheese, round, 1 ... 17
Graham, 4 small or 2 medium squares ... 55
Oyster, 10 ... 45
Rusk, 1 piece ... 50
Rye wafer, crisp, 2 (1⅞ x 3½ inches) ... 45
Saltine, 2 (2-inch square) ... 35
Soda, 2 (2½-inch square) ... 50
Wheat wafer, 1 ... 9
Cranberry juice cocktail
Canned, 1 cup ... 165
Low-cal, 1 cup ... 60
Cranberry sauce, sweetened, canned, 1 cup ... 300

Pie, 1/6 of 9-inch pie
Apple ... 410
Cherry ... 418
Custard ... 327
Lemon meringue ... 357
Mince ... 434
Pumpkin ... 317
Pimiento, canned, 1 medium ... 10
Pineapple
Canned
Heavy syrup, 1 large slice and syrup ... 90
Juice pack, 1 large slice and juice ... 58
Water pack, 1 large slice ... 39
Fresh, diced, ½ cup ... 40
Pizza, cheese, ⅛ of 14-inch pie ... 185
Plums
Canned, ½ cup ... 100
Fresh, 1 (2-inch diameter) ... 25
Popcorn, 1 cup ... 65
Popover, home recipe, 1 average ... 112
Pomegranate, raw, 1 medium ... 63
Pork, cooked
Blade steak, 3½ ounces ... 277
Chop, loin center cut, lean only, 3½ ounces ... 250
Picnic shoulder, fresh, 3½ ounces ... 246
Sausage, cooked, links or patty, 3½ ounces ... 421
Tenderloin, 3½ ounces ... 239
Potato chips, 10 medium ... 115
Potato salad, ½ cup ... 99
Potatoes
Baked, 1 medium ... 90
Boiled, 1 medium ... 80
French fried 10 medium ... 155
Frozen, oven heated, 10 medium ... 125
Hash-browned, ½ cup ... 225
Mashed with milk, ½ cup ... 63
Sweet
Baked, 1 medium ... 155
Candied, 1 medium ... 295
Canned, ½ cup ... 118
Pretzels, 5 small sticks ... 20
Prune juice, canned, 1 cup ... 200

Prunes, dried, cooked, unsweetened, ½ cup ... 148
Pudding, cornstarch
Butterscotch, ½ cup ... 207
Chocolate, ½ cup ... 219
Vanilla, ½ cup ... 152
Pumpkin, canned, 1 cup ... 75

R
Radishes, raw, 4 small ... 5
Raisins, 1 cup ... 460
Raspberries
Black, fresh, ½ cup ... 50
Red, fresh, ½ cup ... 35
Red, frozen, sweetened, ½ cup ... 120
Rhubarb, cooked, sweetened, ½ cup ... 193
Rice, brown, cooked, ½ cup ... 88
Rice, white, cooked, ½ cup ... 82
Roll
Hamburger, 1 medium ... 89
Hard, 1 medium ... 109
Plain, 1 medium ... 113
Sweet, 1 medium ... 178
Romaine, raw, 3½ ounces ... 18
Rutabagas, cooked, ½ cup ... 35

S
Salad dressing
Blue cheese, 1 tablespoon ... 71
Low-cal, 1 tablespoon ... 11
French, 1 tablespoon ... 57
Low-cal, 1 tablespoon ... 13
Home-cooked, 1 tablespoon ... 23
Italian, 1 tablespoon ... 77
Low-cal, 1 tablespoon ... 6
Mayonnaise, 1 tablespoon ... 101
Mayonnaise-type, 1 tablespoon ... 61
Low-cal, 1 tablespoon ... 19
Thousand Island, 1 tablespoon ... 70
Low-cal, 1 tablespoon ... 25
Salad oil, 1 tablespoon ... 125
Sandwich, 1 slice white bread
Bacon, lettuce, tomato ... 282
Chicken salad ... 245
Egg salad ... 279
Ham ... 281
Peanut butter ... 328
Roast beef, hot, with 3 tablespoons gravy ... 429

Fish, cont.

Sardines, canned in oil, 3 ounces...... 175
Swordfish, broiled, 3 ounces...... 150

Tuna
Canned in oil, ½ cup...... 160
Canned in water, ½ cup...... 127
Casserole with noodles, 1 serving...... 280

Fish stick, breaded, 1 serving...... 170
Flour, wheat, all-purpose, enriched, 1 cup sifted...... 400
Flour, wheat, all-purpose, enriched, 1 tablespoon...... 25
Frankfurter, cooked, 1...... 140
Fruit cocktail, canned with syrup, ½ cup...... 100

G

Garlic bulbs, peeled, 1 bulb...... 2

Gelatin dessert
Fruit added, ready-to-serve, ½ cup...... 80
Plain, ready-to-serve, ½ cup...... 70

Gelatin, dry, unflavored, 1 tablespoon...... 35
Ginger ale, 1 cup...... 80
Gooseberries, raw, ⅔ cup...... 39

Grapefruit
Canned, sections, white, with syrup, ½ cup...... 90
Fresh
Pink, ½ medium...... 60
White, ½ medium...... 55
Juice
Fresh, 1 cup...... 100
Sweetened
Canned, 1 cup...... 100
Frozen, reconstituted, 1 cup...... 130
Unsweetened
Canned, 1 cup...... 100
Frozen, reconstituted, 1 cup...... 120

Grapes
Concord, fresh, ½ cup...... 33
Green, fresh, ½ cup...... 48
Juice, canned, 1 cup...... 160

Gravy
Beef, canned, ¼ cup...... 30
Beef, home recipe, ¼ cup...... 60

Griddle cake
Plain, 1 (4-inch diameter)...... 60
Buckwheat, 1 (4-inch diameter)...... 55

H-J

Ham, fully cooked, 3½ ounces...... 219
Hard sauce, 2 tablespoons...... 97
Honey, 1 tablespoon...... 65
Honeydew melon, ¼ small (5-inch diameter)...... 40
Ice cream, vanilla, 10% fat (½ quart)...... 131
Ice milk, (½ quart)...... 103
Jam, grape, 1 tablespoon...... 59
Jelly, 1 tablespoon...... 55

K-M

Kohlrabi, cooked, ½ cup...... 20

Lamb, cooked
Loin chop, 3½ ounces...... 223
Rib chop, 3½ ounces...... 291
Roast leg, center cut, 3½ ounces...... 182
Roast leg, whole, 3½ ounces...... 195

Lard, 1 tablespoon...... 126
Lemon, 1 medium...... 20
Lemon juice, 1 tablespoon...... 5
Lemonade, frozen, sweetened, reconstituted, 1 cup...... 110

Lettuce
Boston, ¼ medium head...... 8
Iceberg, ¼ medium compact head...... 10
Leaves, 2 large or 4 small...... 15

Lime, raw, 1 medium...... 28
Lime juice, 1 tablespoon...... 4
Liverwurst, 2 ounces (3-inch diameter, ¼ inch thick)...... 175

Lobster
Canned, ½ cup...... 75
Newburg, 1 serving...... 194
Thermidor, 1 lobster in shell...... 405

Luncheon meat
Bologna, 1 thin slice (4-inch diameter)...... 86

Luncheon meat, cont.
Ham, boiled, 1 ounce...... 68
Salami, 1 slice (3¾-inch diameter, ¼ inch thick)...... 130

Macaroni, cooked, ½ cup...... 78
Macaroni and cheese, baked, ½ cup...... 235
Malted milk, 1 cup...... 280
Maple syrup, 1 tablespoon...... 50
Margarine, 1 tablespoon...... 100
Marmalade, orange, 1 tablespoon...... 56
Marshmallows, 1 ounce...... 90
Meat loaf, beef and pork, 1 slice (4x3x3/8 inch)...... 264
Melba toast, 1 thin slice...... 15

Milk
Buttermilk, 1 cup...... 90
Chocolate drink, 1 cup...... 190
Condensed, sweetened, undiluted, ½ cup...... 490
Dried, nonfat, instant, 1 cup...... 246
Evaporated, skim, undiluted, ½ cup...... 86
Evaporated, whole, undiluted, ½ cup...... 160
Skim, 1 cup...... 88
Skim, fortified, 1 cup...... 105
Skim, 2% fat, 1 cup...... 147
Whole, 1 cup...... 160

Molasses, light, 1 tablespoon...... 50

Muffin
Blueberry, 1 average (2¾-inch diameter)...... 112
Corn, 1 (2¾-inch diameter)...... 150
Plain, 1 (2¾-inch diameter)...... 140

Mushrooms
Canned, solids and liquids, ½ cup...... 17
Fresh, 10 small or 4 large...... 28

Mussels, 3½ ounces...... 95
Mustard, prepared, 1 tablespoon...... 12

N-O

Nectarines, raw, 2 medium...... 64
Noodles, cooked, ½ cup...... 100

Nuts
Almonds, dried, salted, unblanched, 13 to 15...... 105
Brazil nuts, 4...... 97
Cashews, roasted, 4 to 5...... 95

Nuts, cont.
Peanuts, roasted, shelled, chopped, 1 tablespoon...... 55
Pecans, chopped, 1 tablespoon...... 50
Walnuts, chopped, 1 tablespoon...... 50

Okra, cooked, 8 pods (3x5/8 inch)...... 25
Olives, green, 4 medium...... 15
Olives, ripe, 3 small...... 15

Onion
Cooked, ½ cup...... 30
Green, 6 small without tops...... 20
Mature, raw, chopped, 1 tablespoon...... 5

Orange
Mature, raw, 1 medium...... 75

Orange juice
Canned, unsweetened, 1 cup...... 120
Fresh, 1 cup...... 115
Frozen, reconstituted, 1 cup...... 110

Oyster stew, 1 cup (3 to 4 oysters)...... 200
Oysters, raw, ½ cup (6 to 10 medium)...... 80

P

Pancake, 1 average (4-inch diameter)...... 60
Parsley, raw, 3½ ounces...... 4
Parsnips, cooked, ½ cup...... 50

Peaches
Canned, 2 medium halves and 2 tablespoons syrup...... 90
Frozen, sweetened, ½ cup...... 105
Fresh, 1 medium...... 35

Pears
Canned, 2 medium halves and 2 tablespoons syrup...... 90
Fresh, 1 medium...... 100

Peanut butter, 1 tablespoon...... 95
Peas, green, cooked, ½ cup...... 58
Pepper, green, raw, 1 medium...... 10
Pickle relish, sour, 3½ ounces...... 19
Pickle relish, sweet, 3½ ounces...... 138

Pickles
Dill, 1 large (4x1¾ inch)...... 15
Sweet, 1 medium (2¾x¾ inch)...... 30

HOW TO LIVE WITH YOUR DIET

1. Think of your diet as a time for developing new eating habits that will become a way of life for you. Once you reach your desired weight, adjust your eating habits to maintain your new weight.

2. Set realistic goals for yourself before starting your diet. Decide how many pounds you want to lose within a certain period of time, then plan your diet accordingly.

3. Learn to separate hunger from appetite. Less food is needed to satisfy hunger than appetite. Don't eat when you're not hungry.

4. Accept the fact that you may frequently experience hunger as you begin your diet.

5. Eat meals which are nutritionally balanced. Avoid crash diets based upon a specific food or group of foods as they are often nutritionally unsound and lack variety.

6. Space your meals according to individual preference. If you prefer to eat more often than 3 times a day, divide your daily food allowance into several smaller meals.

7. Eat a wide variety of foods to keep your diet interesting. Well-planned menus can often include a favorite higher calorie food.

8. Include as many fresh fruits and vegetables in your diet as possible. Uncooked foods are higher in bulk and so, provide a more filled-up feeling at the end of a meal.

9. Select low-calorie foods that allow a moderate-sized serving without going over your allotted calorie allowance. Pass up second helpings and avoid foods that are so high in calories that the serving portion is discouragingly small.

10. Plan at least one food in each meal which can be eaten in an unlimited amount, such as lettuce, celery, mushrooms, cucumber, green pepper, radishes, cabbage, broccoli, cauliflower, or spinach.

11. Take advantage of commercially prepared low-calorie foods. They add variety to meals and make available some foods which are otherwise not possible on a diet.

12. Reserve part of your meal, such as the appetizer, salad, or dessert course for an afternoon or late-evening snack.

13. Eat slowly to allow more time to savor each morsel. Avoid eating your meals in tense or hectic surroundings.

14. Reward yourself as you reach each pre-established weight loss goal. Avoid using food as a reward. Instead, purchase a new piece of clothing or additional equipment for a favorite hobby or sport.

15. Recognize that weight loss is generally unsteady and is not always noticeable for the first several days of your diet. Weigh every few days in the morning before eating or drinking. Avoid keeping a daily weight chart since weight loss is not always reflected on a day-to-day basis.

16. Get plenty of sleep, particularly the first few weeks of your diet. You are less likely to stray from your diet or yield to temptation when you are mentally alert.

17. Increase your physical activity to use up excess calories. Include many and varied activities that keep you busy and prevent idle snacking or thinking of food.

18. Keep high-calorie snack foods out of sight. Instead, select wholesome foods rather than those which merely add calories.

19. Maintain your social activities in keeping with your new eating habits. Do not forego social pleasures just because you're counting calories, but learn to adjust these activities in a realistic manner.

20. Live your diet—don't just talk about it or monopolize family conversation with it.

INDEX